WOMEN, PUBLIC OPINION, AND POLITICS

WOMEN, PUBLIC OPINION, AND POLITICS

The Changing Political Attitudes of American Women

Keith T. Poole
Carnegie-Mellon University

L. Harmon Zeigler
University of Oregon

Longman
New York and London

WOMEN, PUBLIC OPINION, AND POLITICS
The Changing Political Attitudes
of American Women

Longman Inc., 1560 Broadway, New York, N.Y. 10036
Associated companies, branches, and representatives
throughout the world.

Copyright © 1985 by Longman Inc.

All rights reserved. No part of this publication may be
reproduced, stored in a retrieval system, or transmitted
in any form or by any means, electronic, mechanical,
photocopying, recording, or otherwise, without the prior
permission of the publisher.

Developmental Editor: Irving E. Rockwood
Editorial and Design Supervisor: Barbara Lombardo
Production Supervisor: Ferne Y. Kawahara
Composition: Times Printing, Inc.
Printing and Binding: Malloy Lithographing, Inc.

Library of Congress Cataloging in Publication Data

Poole, Keith T.
  Women, public opinion, and politics.

  Includes index.
  1. Women—United States—Attitudes. 2. Women in
politics—United States. 3. Women—United States—
Social conditions. 4. United States—Politics and
government—1981- —Public opinion. 5. Public
opinion—United States. 6. Women—United States—Public opinion.
I. Zeigler, L. Harmon (Luther Harmon), 1936— II. Title.
HQ1410.P66   1985   305.4'0973   84-7155
ISBN 0-582-28274-8
ISBN 0-582-28273-X (pbk.)

Manufactured in the United States of America
Printing: 9 8 7 6 5 4 3 2 1   Year: 92 91 90 89 88 87 86 85

Contents

Foreword		vii
Preface		xi
Chapter 1	**Introduction**	1
	The Experience of Work	7
	Education and Attitudes of Women toward Equality	13
	Support for the Women's Liberation Movement	20
	Life Satisfaction and Work	25
	Feminism: Diffusion, Awareness, and Constraint	31
Chapter 2	**Women and the Vote: An Overview of Recent Presidential Elections**	**41**
	Issue Saliency in 1980	54
	Issue Saliency and the Vote in 1980	57
	Attitudes on the Issues and the Vote in 1980	60
	1980: Mandate for Reagan or Rejection of Carter?	79
	Gender and the Vote in 1980	85
	Beyond the Gender Gap	85
Chapter 3	**Ideology and the Attitudes of Women in 1980**	**95**
	Introduction	95
	Ideology and Women's Issues	98
	Other Issues	110
	Conclusion	116

Chapter 4	**Political Participation**	**121**
	Partisanship and Participation	127
	Trust and Cynicism	129
	Trust and Participation	135
	Efficacy	136
	If Everyone Voted Would It Change Anything?	140
	Conclusion	147
Chapter 5	**Women in the House of Representatives**	**151**
	Introduction	151
	Women Members Are More Liberal Than Men	154
	Party Loyalty of Men and Women	156
	Issues That Separate the Parties	158
	Conclusion	173
	Appendix A	**179**
	Appendix B	**183**
	Index	191

Foreword

During the past decade the growing number of scholars in political science who are women have shared an open secret: that topics concerning women and politics present a goldmine for academic researchers. The political participation patterns of American women—roughly half the population and now equal to men in voter turnout—have regularly been ignored or dismissed by insertions of hackneyed stereotypes even in the major works of the discipline. With the present study Keith Poole and Harmon Zeigler join their efforts to those of the talented scholars mining this rich vein.

Poole and Zeigler project a startling vision. They anticipate that women will continue to lack the kind of group cohesion that characterizes blacks. However, the authors assert that growing numbers of women voters who are tending to combine particular liberal commitments will carry the American political system to the left in the coming decades. All the more interesting is the authors' conclusion that, apart from women's unity on discrete issues affecting them, the range of their values and attitudes offer major opportunities for both the Democratic and Republican parties.

The nature and impact of the modern women's movement is debatable. Are the changing lives of women attributable to the movement's influence or to the severe fluctuations of the economic system? Is there a women's movement in the 1980's? Whatever the reasons, the attitudinal data indicates that college educated employed women clearly embrace the egalitarian attitudes which the women's movement introduced. This cohort accepts an interpretation of liberalism distinctively its own and not to be confused with the understanding professed by liberal men and liberal housewives. These relatively privileged women, like other liberals, accept the standard notions of government intervention in the economy. To that they have also affixed their expectation that government must advance the conditions for women's equality. Poole and Zeigler underline the strong differences that separate these women and traditional women. But they also perceive evidence over the past ten to fifteen years that these privileged women's views have begun to penetrate through the broader female population. The result is that lesser educated but employed women are increasingly receptive to egalitarianism despite their lingering hesitations about feminist organizations. Even the hostile attitudes of housewives have moderated at least to a degree.

Moderation is the byword of the women's movement today. The data which the authors have reviewed indicates that the women's movement has matured and stabilized with the prospect of becoming an established player in American political life. While the moderation which accompanies such a mainstream status will disappoint feminists on the left, the resulting amalgam will be all the more attractive to large numbers of women. Trends in women's education and their employment solidify this phenomenon. Women now make up the majority of the student bodies in colleges and universities. Over a majority of all women are employed. While education is the critical factor in changing women's relationship to politics, employment leads to women's increased sense of efficacy in public affairs. Their developing political sophistication in conjunction with the limited economic opportunities projected for them, would seem to yield a sharpened sense of shared interest.

All of this points toward unity; yet diffusion is also characteristic of women's political positions. The authors' examination of issue saliency for women reveals the conservative leanings of significant numbers of women who support school prayer, federal budget restraint, skepticism about government job creation programs and receptivity to the maintenance of reenforced defense systems. The stereotype of women as soft-hearted is challenged by the significant numbers of women who oppose bussing, object to help for minorities and reject abortion choice. Republicans will find a receptive constituency here. Democrats, on the other hand, should be interested to learn that, among many of the same women who are skeptical of social programs, a pattern of support exists for environmental protection, rapprochement with the Russians and opposition to nuclear power. With such crosscurrents of interests within an increasingly active and discriminating group of voters both parties will need to do more than rely on traditional appeals. Given feminists' efforts to attack the traditional treatment of sex as a class, hard evidence showing the crosscurrents of values, attitudes and interests among women is significant. The implications of Poole's and Zeigler findings should provoke caution in any who claim to speak for women on other than gender related issues.

While the subject of this study is women's political attitudes and behavior, an obscure but interesting subtheme treats men's attitudes on issues of egalitarianism. Evidently education, the major influence on women's thinking about equality, has no perceptible impact on men's thinking about these questions. Despite this pattern men are more supportive of the E.R.A. than housewives. Whereas men's voting patterns can be explained by their employment, women's voting choices are revealed by their educational level. Any number of important questions arise about how the educational experiences of men and women yield such differing results. The phenomenon of men holding more egalitarian attitudes on women's behalf than traditional women deserves a closer look.

With the gender gap entering our political lexicon, Poole and Zeigler offer new angles for us to ponder. The most interesting gap is not the often exaggerated and, to date, unreliable gap between male and female voters. Poole and Zeigler identify a widening chasm between the perspectives of employed women and housewives whose declining numbers hint at becoming an exotic statistical category. The regular growth in the numbers of working women and women's strong response to higher education is yielding a sophisticated electorate ready to combine on gender questions such as the E.R.A. and abortion choice but equally ready to go separate ways on nongender issues. At the same time antifeminism has gained powerful backing particularly from wealthy fundamentalist churches committed to maintaining traditional sex roles. Politics in the coming decade will be imprinted by the tension between feminist— whatever its source—and antifeminist positions.

Who will find the Poole and Zeigler study useful? Anyone who needs to know what changes are taking place in American politics or in the lives of American women. While useful for courses on women and politics, voting behavior, and political socialization; it should be of no less interest to Democratic and Republican Party leadership both on the state and national levels. The fundamental political changes documented here are potentially equal in significance to the consequences of the more widely publicized and better understood technological revolution.

Michele Shover
California State University, Chico

Preface

This book is a study of the political attitudes of American women. Most of the book deals with mass attitudes. We are especially concerned with the relationship between attitudes toward equality for women and attitudes about other issues, such as regulating the environment, defense spending, and the like.

Since the book is about mass opinions, only passing attention is given to attitudes of female elites, those who represent women through various feminist organizations. Our focus upon the "foot soldiers" presents information at variance with media descriptions of women's political beliefs. We believe women's attitudes are understood from an examination of the structure of beliefs among the masses, not from the pronouncements of group leaders.

We begin by describing how women feel about equality and the women's movement. We then address the ability of women to link these very focused attitudes toward more general beliefs, and the ability of women to link both sets of beliefs with candidate preference.

Our next concern is with *constraint*, that puzzling concept describing one's ability to develop a belief system—to connect disparate attitudes into a coherent value system.

Our final section on mass opinion and behavior concerns political participation, with the variables used in the previous discussion employed to understand variance in voting and other forms of participation.

We conclude with an analysis of women in the House of Representatives. Women are participating more in politics and surely they will ultimately occupy their fair share of elected offices. Assuming this to be the case, we deem it prudent to understand the dimensions of congressional voting.

The book is not about the feminist social movement. It does not directly address the development of women's organizations, but focuses upon the response of typical women to what has happened to them in their name.

The data are drawn, with rare exceptions, from the national election studies conducted by the Institute for Social and Political Research at the University of Michigan.

We are grateful to the Inter-University Consortium for Political and Social Research for providing us with the data. We are more grateful to those scholars who preceded us and enlightened us with excellent examinations of similar sets of data: Claire Fulenwider, Virginia Sapiro, Sandra Baxter, and Marjorie Lansing. Our debt to them is obvious. We offer to Virginia Sapiro our thanks for the best evaluation of a manuscript we have ever encountered. It hurt but it helped. It need hardly be added that none of the flaws in the book are her responsibility, only the good parts.

1
Introduction

Writing about the political attitudes and behavior of women is an enterprise both difficult and relatively new. If one examines the standard texts, monographs, and articles reflecting the collective wisdom of political science for the last 20 years, one might conclude that women are not different from men. In some cases, writers add an occasional comment that women are, in fact, not distinguishable as a group. In other cases, the assumption goes unsaid.

The reasons for this neglect are not solely attributable to the fact that most political scientists are men. Most political scientists are not black, lower class, or Republican. Yet race, class, and partisan identification form the eternal triangle of political analysis. The reasons for the neglect of women as a group are more complex, and less conspiratorial. Discrimination against women has deep historical roots, but the acknowledgment that such discrimination is inappropriate is a recent development. Generally speaking, women were not regarded as a politically relevant group until the feminist movement of the middle and late 1960s. In contrast, racial discrimination has been generally deplored for more than a century, and black organizations to combat racism are as old. Consequently, analysis of the political attitudes and behaviors of blacks is well established.

The movement to achieve women's suffrage focused primarily upon the right to vote. Once the right to vote had been won the women's suffrage movement lost momentum. Success often leads to apathy in interest groups with a single cause. Consequently, Jo

Freeman remarks that "sometime during the 1920s, feminism died in the United States."[1] Freeman's lament may be slightly exaggerated. Like most social movements, the struggle for sexual equity has gone through a variety of phases. After winning the right to vote, organizations representing women lost the unity they had previously developed. The League of Women Voters and the National Association of Business and Professional Women were active in promoting various causes not generally regarded as feminist, while the National Women's Party first proposed the Equal Rights Amendment in 1923.

Clearly the surge of feminist activity beginning in the late 1960s was not without historical precedent, but it is certainly possible to make a distinction between the "new feminism" of today and the "old feminism" surrounding the passage of the Nineteenth Amendment.[2] For example, the National Organization for Women (NOW), one of the most active feminist organizations, is in its infancy. It was formed in 1966, two years after the passage of the Civil Rights Act, and five years after the establishment by President John F. Kennedy of a Commission on the Status of Women.

The relative infancy of the new feminist movement is also due to the general acceptance, by women and men, of the notion of *legitimate discrimination*. Discrimination has become a pejorative word. However, there is no denying that some discrimination is acceptable. Grade school children do not vote in public elections; teenagers and other youthful employees are given a modicum of special protection, and so on. Until recently, discrimination against women was, if not acceptable, certainly not regarded as serious a problem as discrimination against minorities. The perceived need for special protection, the belief that women were in some manner more vulnerable than men, led many women's organizations into initial opposition to the Equal Rights Amendment (ERA). Boles notes that the ERA opponents were still supportive of protection and special privileges for women.[3] Inequality was supported by a variety of cultural norms and social institutions. Schools, mass media, and especially families contributed to gender role stereotyping, the major focus of which was to limit the role of the "successful" woman to that of housewife.

In television commercials, and in the entertainment segments, for example, women are portrayed frequently as homemakers; a far greater proportion of women on TV work only as homemakers than the proportion of women who are, in reality, exclusively involved in the care of children and the maintenance of a home. Although at least half of real American families have two incomes, it is invariably the TV woman who becomes distressed when her husband complains about the coffee, or his dirty shirt.

Since the woman's role was solely to be in the home, success and failure for women were narrowly defined. As Glazer explains, "The failure to marry or failure in marriage is a total failure for many women, while for men it is only a partial failure. Marriage defines a woman's role and her appropriate social character."[4] Politically, women were defined according to the characteristics of their husbands. Working class women voted for Democrats; upper class women voted for Republicans. Most white women did not live in ghettos; did not have to sit at the back of the bus; never saw a drinking fountain reserved for men. It was far more serious for a social or business organization to exclude black men than to exclude women.

Most women themselves accepted these roles without serious reservation. A frequent manifestation of docility was the willingness of women to conceal intellectual skills in order to avoid threatening men. Women who refused and were able to achieve professional success outside the home were viewed with suspicion. Voluntary docility (the *fear of success syndrome*) was so subtle and pervasive, that it went without serious challenge.[5]

In terms of sheer intensity, the response to discrimination against blacks has been far more severe than has the response to discrimination against women. Blacks and whites were killed at a time when *Playboy* magazine ran advertisements for men's ties with pigs (symbolizing a male chauvinist pig). Equality for women was not high on the public agenda. Discrimination against women was trivialized as inconsequential while discrimination against blacks was causing death. It is unlikely one would have been able to buy a tie with KKK on it.

The upshot of all of this is to suggest that there are intellectual and methodological problems in treating women as a group, because they do not appear to be as cohesive in their attitudes as do, for example, blacks. Consider the following situation. Suppose you were asked to look at two people, one a black (either man or woman) and the other a woman (white). Now suppose that on the basis of this observation alone you were required to bet $100 on your ability to guess how each voted in the 1980 presidential election. If you bet that the black voted for Carter, your probability of success is about 90 percent, a good bet. If you bet that the woman voted for Carter, your probability of success is no better than 50 percent. In other words, blacks voted as a bloc and women did not. In fact, since the establishment of the Roosevelt coalition in the 1930s, blacks have voted Democratic at about an 80 percent rate, whereas women have shown no clear preference for either party.

In 1980, a candidate running on a platform of opposition to the Equal Rights Amendment and in favor of a constitutional amendment prohibiting abortions (Reagan) split the women's vote with a candidate who supported the Equal Rights Amendment and, albeit reluctantly, opposed the abortion amendment (Carter). One could argue, of course, that the choice was between the lesser of two evils; NOW did not endorse Carter because of his alleged failure to pursue with vigor the goals espoused by feminist organizations.

On the surface, then, it appears that there is an absence of group cohesion among women. Women do not appear to be a political group; there are no political attitudes and behaviors which are unique to them *as women*. Obviously, in the categoric sense of the word, women are a group (as are people over 6 feet tall, people with blonde hair, and so on). But do they behave as an interest group? David Truman's aging but valid definition of a political interest group is unusually relevant here. *Do women, on the basis of "shared attitudes," pursue public policy goals implied by the shared attitudes?*[6] Why should they? Certainly men are not a political group. Men do not act upon the basis of shared attitudes, because there are none.

White males suffer substantially less economic discrimination than women, suggesting perhaps that economic discrimination can serve to strengthen the group consciousness of women. This may be, but the problem of organizing people with similar economic problems according to consensual or common attitudes is hardly unique. Who is, for example, the worker? Who speaks for the working class? Is it the AFL-CIO? No more than one-fourth of the work force is unionized. Even among the unionized segment, union lobbyists frequently misrepresent their clientele. Union leaders endorsed George McGovern, but many rank and file members preferred another George—Wallace of Alabama. Who speaks for the consumer? Isn't everyone a consumer?

Group consciousness is a valuable political resource, assuming that it can be articulated by group leaders. For women, this resource is not yet as developed as it is for blacks, even though the weight of economic discrimination on women is heavier. Black males have now inched ahead of women in annual income. But collective response is relatively new. At the early stages of the feminist movement, considerable attention was given to the problems of women and there was possibly more attitude cohesion. Whether or not such efforts succeeded, the fact that they were made indicates the extent to which group consciousness has been, and continues to be, a problem. In Truman's terms, the cross-cutting claims of other identifications minimize shared attitudes. It cannot be emphasized strongly enough that problems of cross-cutting identifications, low attitudinal cohesion, and, consequently, relatively poor ability for organizations to convert attitudes into action are not the sole domain of women.

In addition to the obvious examples discussed earlier, one can point to smaller groups which *should* have great cohesion. Consider, for example, physicians. Publicly, the American Medical Association (AMA) represented them as believing Medicare was the first step toward socialism. However, surveys of physicians revealed that a majority were *not* opposed to Medicare. There were intragroup conflicts among general practitioners, specialists in clinics, pathologists working in large hospitals, and medical researchers committed to preventive medicine. If physicians, all of whom have undergone a narrow and constraining recruitment process, do not agree, then surely one cannot expect agreement in such a broad group as women.

On the other hand, there is no denying the fact that women should, and perhaps in time will, develop more group consciousness. Although they have not experienced a pattern of socialization as constraining as that of physicians, until recently women have had fewer occupational choices and, had a more uniform path to adulthood than men. All women, whatever else they do not have in common, are likely to be more responsible for raising children than men are, given past and present gender role stereotyping. It is certainly true that, with the massive entry of women into the workforce, household responsibilities are more likely to be shared. However, even with a husband and wife employed, men have not assumed an equal burden in the home.[7] Women bear children; men do not. And women have primary responsibility for child care in most homes. This is not to suggest that women are naturally more inclined toward a nurturing role. Indeed, the most comprehensive study on sex differences currently available, Eleanor Macoby's *The Psychology of Sex Differences,* concludes that there is *little hard evidence to equate "maternal" behavior with genetic sex differences.* Anthropologists can cite examples of societies in which men are charged with the mother role. Nevertheless, women generally assume a major role in family matters.

According to popular stereotypes, this common experience should make women more humane, pacific, and gentle. Generally, such expectations have not been fulfilled. However, one can point to evidence in support of the common background of their maternal roles leading to common interests among women. Women are more concerned with and active in local educational politics. They also populate school boards at a rate far higher than they populate other governmental bodies. One could infer that, since schools share with women the responsibility for child welfare, such high interest and activity is an extension of women's family role.

Like most potentially active people, women become engaged in politics at the point of greatest salience. Poor blacks, once portrayed as ignorant of the political process, know the intricacies of welfare and poverty implementation better than those who do not encounter the welfare bureaucracy. To return to our betting exercise, if you were required to bet another $100 upon which of two people, one a man and one a woman, was more likely to be a local school activist, a bet on the woman would not be going against the odds.

The odds become poorer if one tries to infer a more general set of attitudes derived from the family responsibilities of women. Majorities of men *and* women oppose busing to achieve racial equality, reduction of defense spending, legal abortions under any circumstances; majorities of both sexes favor the death penalty. On the other hand, women do seem more inclined to eschew the use of force. Women were more likely than men to have been "doves" during the Vietnam war, irrespective of whether or not a woman was ideologically attracted to feminism. Additionally, irrespective of their views about feminism, women were more loath to resort to force in the event of urban unrest. However, women were not more hostile to the recent registration of males for a potential draft (although they were less inclined than men to support the registration of women). There appears to be some marginal differences between men and women, but, over the broad array of issues that rise and fall during the political lives of women and men, the similarities far exceed the differences. Virginia Sapiro concludes that there is "no consistent indication that women are either clearly more or less feminist than are men"[8] on issues of special interest to women (e.g., those dealing with sex discrimination).

The last 15 years have seen feminist organizations pursue feminist goals with highly visible vigor. The fight for and against ratification of the Equal Rights Amendment achieved national attention in part because of a NOW-supported boycott of all nonratified states. The struggle for legal abortion engages the emotion of countless advocates and opponents. *Can it be possible that these struggles are waged between two elites, with the mass of women relatively uninvolved? It is not only possible, but highly probable.* Public policies are typically enacted because of elite activity, and the most visible feminist issues are not an exception to this rule. In truth, despite the substantial media attention given to feminist causes, the majority of both men and women do not assign high priority to such issues; they are more concerned with broadly based economic problems.

All of which suggests that a book about women as a political group is neither desirable nor possible. *We propose instead to subject women to the same sort of analysis as men are routinely subjected to. The dimensions of class, education, and occupation, for example, differentiate women as clearly as they do men.* If women are not a uniform political group, then there are groups of women. Employed women differ from housewives, the rich differ from the poor, the educated are different from the less fortunate, and so on. To pursue the illusion of women as a monolithic group is to neglect the fact of their great diversity. We propose to study this diversity.

THE EXPERIENCE OF WORK

Our analysis begins with the experience of work outside the home, an experience common to men but not, until recently, to women. The percentage of women in the labor force has been steadily increasing. More than one-half of all women, married and single, are now employed outside the home. It is probable that the percentage of employed women will continue to increase, as inflation and continued worsening of economic conditions make two paychecks essential.

One should expect this burgeoning population of employed women to be more in sympathy with the goals of feminism than housewives. One major feminist argument is that women must be liberated from traditional roles; certainly the most traditional of such roles is that of housewife. Therefore, those who are not solely housewives should be more attuned to the ideology of feminism. Housewives should be less inclined toward feminism because they are, whether consciously or unconsciously, socialized into a position of lowered expectations. It may also be true that housewives are reluctant to risk the uncertainties of employment in exchange for the uncertainties of unemployment. The attitude of feminist leaders toward housewives has been ambivalent.[9] Feminist organizations appear to address the needs of employed women, most urgently. In some cases, the designation of traditional roles has led more passionate feminists to equate housewives with slaves, a comparison which probably does not sit well with women who remain in the home. If housewives are made uncertain about the value of their lives, they may react with hostility to egalitarian ideologies, or at least to the most visible proponents of egalitarianism. Hence, such clichés as "I'm in favor of equality but can't stand women's libbers" are often heard. It is certainly true that preoccupation with home and family can isolate a woman from the mainstream of political participation, and the self-esteem of housewives may have been a casualty of the feminist movement.

Threats to self-esteem may be perceived in proposals to alter the traditional relationship of men and women, even if no threats were intended. However, such threats should be less apparent among employed women, who have already altered these relationships. The simple act of leaving the home, for whatever reason, should sensitize the employed woman to the rude facts of discrimination and to the desirability of change.

Beginning in 1972, the Survey Research Center included in its national election studies a set of questions which asked respondents to place themselves along a seven-point scale. The scale was intended to assess the respondent's commitment to equality for women. Accordingly, those who placed themselves at position one agreed that "women and men should have an equal role" and those who placed themselves at position seven believed that "women's place is in the home."

Figure 1.1 displays the distributions of housewives and employed women over the scale from 1972 to 1980. (Only portions of the complete data set are shown in the figure. See Appendix B for a detailed presentation.) Juxtaposing cross-sectional and panel data is necessary to show not only how attitudes are changing over time, but also to study the changing mix of employed women and housewives in the surveys. In 1972, 47 percent of the women in the sample identified themselves as housewives. By 1976, this percentage had fallen to 37 percent, and by 1982 it had fallen to 28 percent—a drop of nearly 20 percentage points in just eight years! The flip side of the coin is the percentage of women identifying themselves as employed. They increased from 39 percent in 1972 to 48 percent in 1982. In the panel study, which began in 1972, of the 277 women identifying themselves as housewives, 65 had switched to identifying themselves as employed women by 1976. In fact, only 178 of the original 277 (or 64 percent) thought of themselves as housewives by 1976! The remaining 34 were either retired, unemployed, or were

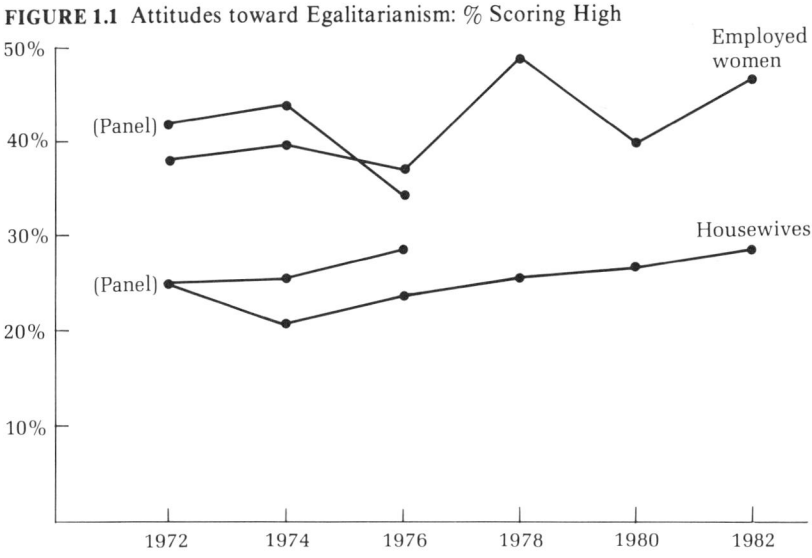

FIGURE 1.1 Attitudes toward Egalitarianism: % Scoring High

students. In contrast, 73 percent of the women who were employed in 1972 were still employed in 1976 (188 of 259). Only 31 employed women switched to being housewives by 1976. In sum, 23 percent of the employed women returned to the home. In Figure 1.1, we have displayed only the housewives and employed women whose status did not change and who were interviewed at all three time points.

In 1972, when the question was initially asked, employed women were more egalitarian (and less traditional) than housewives. The percentage of housewives placing themselves at the extreme egalitarian position has remained relatively steady, around 25 percent in the cross-sectional surveys. This constancy does not mean that equality for women is not making inroads among housewives. Support for the extreme traditionalist position has fallen sharply, from 29 percent to 12 percent. The discarding of this position occurs most dramatically between 1972 and 1974, after which there is some backsliding. Even taking this slight tendency to return to traditional values into account, however, the bulk of housewives fall between the extremes; a majority (or, in 1972, a plurality) reject both extreme traditionalism and extreme egalitarianism. Furthermore, although housewives are not enthralled by the prospect of complete equality, they do not fit the stereotype of the slave to housework living in blissful ignorance of oppression. With the exception of 1972, the extreme egalitarian position gains more support than the extreme traditionalist position.

The distribution of housewives in the panel throughout the 1972-1976 period is very similar to that of the housewives in the cross-sectional surveys. The only significant difference between the 1972 and 1976 distributions are the percentages in the moderate-traditionalist and traditionalist categories. As the percentage of women identifying themselves as housewives shrank, those housewives remaining shifted away from extreme traditionalism.

Employed women present a very different picture. Overall, employed women are more egalitarian than housewives. Feminism is more acceptable to them, even without taking into account such additional factors as education or income. Simply getting out of the house contributes to feminism. The 65 women in the panel study who were housewives in 1972 and who entered the workforce by 1976 were more supportive of an equal role for women. Support for extreme and moderate traditionalism fell from 33 percent to 21 percent, while support for extreme and moderate egalitarianism rose from 46 percent to 59 percent. Clearly, once women enter the labor force, they find equality more of a reasonable aspiration than do housewives. For instance, although it is widely believed (and supported by survey data) that women, in general, would prefer to work for a man rather than a woman, this is not the case for women who actually are employed. Employed women are less likely (by a small margin) than men to prefer to work for a male.[10]

From 1972 until 1974, employed women were increasingly enthusiastic about equality. The proportion at the egalitarian extreme increased, while the proportion at the extreme traditional end of the scale decreased. But between 1974 and 1976 the extreme egalitarians lost a portion of their enthusiasm. The lockstep movement of the employed women in the panel study with the employed women in the cross-sectional surveys shows that this decline is real, not simply a sampling fluke. Furthermore, the total support for the two extreme positions declined steadily from 1972 to 1976.

The data after 1976 do not fit as cleanly into this pattern. In 1978, the percentage of employed women placing themselves at the extreme egalitarian position leaped 12 percentage points, from 37 to 49 percent, only to fall back to 40 percent in 1980—and then to increase again to 47 percent in 1982. Unfortunately, there are no panel data after 1976 to compare with the cross-sectional surveys. Nevertheless, some trends emerge clearly.

Support for extreme traditionalism has declined steadily but shows some sign of leveling off. On the other hand, with the exception of employed women in 1978 and 1982, support for extreme egalitarianism has remained fairly stable while support for moderate egalitarianism has increased markedly. However, all of this is complicated by the fact that the percentage of women in the workforce is steadily *increasing*. The panel results suggest that initial exposure to a workplace outside the home produces an early increase in commitment to equality, followed by a drop in support. The sharp rise of support by employed women for extreme egalitarianism in 1978 followed by the lower levels of 1980 and 1982 could, therefore, be due to the large increase of employed women in the 1978 sample.

There are a variety of possible explanations for this movement toward the center (or should we say "left-center"), all with some merits and some deficiencies. The year 1972 was clearly a year in which feminism received maximum publicity. The candidacy of George McGovern, strongly and visibly supported by feminists, drew attention to the inferior economic status of women. The Equal Rights Amendment was endorsed by platforms of both major parties and appeared to be headed for prompt ratification. Feminist organizations were just on the edge of establishing popular name familiarity. Feminist causes were gaining elite support. Abortion was made legal in January 1973. Legislation to implement federal funding of abortions was passed, modified, and ultimately challenged in the courts. The Hyde amendments to the abortion legislation generated highly emotional thrusts and counterthrusts. Additional controversies developed over the implementation of Title VII and affirmative action. Clearly the problem of equity for women was front and center.

By 1974, some of the steam had gone out of the movement. The ERA bogged down after an initial surge. Opposition from conservative women's organizations was partially responsible; Phyllis Schlafly's efforts to halt ratification of the Equal Rights Amendment focused attention upon the division within the ranks of women. Although majorities of both men and women indicated approval of the ERA, the intensity of approval was not high. It was quite easy for Mrs. Schlafly to create the impression of widespread female opposition. Additionally, the attention given to the Equal Rights Amendment spilled over, in the public mind, into the question of abortion, and ultimately into misgivings about the stability and survival of the traditional family. The events Virgina Sapiro warned about came to pass. Without intending to do so, the feminist movement allowed itself to be portrayed as more radical than it actually was. In 1977, 42 percent of women interviewed in a CBS/*New York Times* poll[11] indicated their belief that the women's movement had been a major cause of family breakdown. While these doubts hardly caused a wholesale desertion of feminist aspirations, it is consistent with our data to advance the notion that many women switched to a more moderate view (indicating a few nagging second thoughts). As Sapiro explains, feminist ideology had expanded to include an advocacy of altered male and female roles, possibly creating a threat to female self-esteem.[12] Looking back on the media portrayal of the feminist movement, it is apparent that more attention was devoted to feminist organizations' increasingly comprehensive criticism of sex discrimination and less attention devoted to the emerging moderate view among the clients—potential and actual—of feminist organizations.

Not only was feminist ideology no longer immune to highly visible assault, but women who were employed by 1982 had more personal, less abstract, experiences in the marketplace. The experience of work outside the home, and especially success, tempers women's commitment to doctrinaire ideology and substitutes a more pragmatic view of the world. This is certainly true of our panel of employed women. The falloff from commitment to absolute equality can be explained in this framework. The employed women in the panel were employed; they were getting along. *As is true of most social movements, maturity and moderation were achieved simultaneously.* It is ironic, therefore, that the very activity which contributes to increased sympathy with feminist ideology—work—also contributes to its dilution.

EDUCATION AND ATTITUDES OF WOMEN TOWARD EQUALITY

It is certainly true that women's experience of work is not uniform. Most are employed in traditional women's fields, such as elementary school teaching, nursing, social work, or secretarial work. A glance at the distribution of women by occupation reveals all too clearly that, although gains have been made, women in the workforce are segregated from men. Considering the ratio of women to men, there is egregious underrepresentation of women in the fields of law, medicine, engineering, sales management, and insurance. There is substantial overrepresentation of women in library science, nursing and related fields, precollegiate education, sales clerks, bank tellers, bookkeepers and cashiers, receptionists, telephone operators, and most conspicuously—secretarial work (the ratio of women to men in this field is the highest reported, an astonishing 62.89; the lowest ratio is among engineers, .03).

It is true that education and occupation are as closely related for women as they are for men. The more you learn the more you earn; still, women who are highly educated (college graduates) are far less likely than men of similar education to end up in more desirable occupations. For example, only *nine percent* of women college graduates are classified as managers or administrators, compared to

25 percent of college educated men. In fact, women pay a substantial "gender tax." Seven percent of women with only a high school education are in managerial jobs; thus a college education results in only a slight increase. For men, the relationship is more dramatic; 15 percent of high school graduates are managers and 25 percent of college graduates are managers.[13]

Education is an additional variable in explaining the women's attitudes toward equality. Even though the rewards of education are less apparent for women, they do exist. Educated women are somewhat more likely to end up in better jobs. Thus, using education as a surrogate for more complex indicators of social class is imperfect, but usable.

The importance of moving beyond the rather crude distinction among women based solely upon employment is readily apparent. The feminist movement, since its inception (as is true of most, if not all, social movements), has been the province of the relatively well-to-do. If women are, as a group, less well off than men, it is nevertheless the case that some are more equal than others. Social class has traditionally been based upon a combination of income, education, and subjective class placement. Occupation is also frequently factored in. It is difficult to place women in a social class using these variables. They may be earning very little yet have a high family income. They may be highly educated and be employed in a relatively low status occupation. Unfortunately, the larger notion of social class is not as useful a concept for women as it is for men. When women are regarded as from the working class, it is usually because their husbands are manual laborers.[14]

Numerous other writers on the subject have remarked about the extent to which feminist ideology is more prevalent among the upper classes, irrespective of how class is measured. That this is true should come as no surprise. *Political life in general is disproportionately the hobby of the upper class.* This is especially true when the ideological thrust of the political activity is conventionally liberal, as is certainly the case with feminism. Change is more acceptable to those with higher education. Progressive movements are almost uniformly begun and sustained by the upper strata, even when the movement is designed to liberate the downtrodden. Anthony Oberschall writes of protest movements, "it is difficult to escape the conclusion that the upper and middle strata in society supply the substantial bulk of opposition leaders to all manner of social movements far above that of their percentage in the population at large. . . . The social origins of protest leaders are rather similar to, instead of strikingly different from, the social origins of leaders of established parties with whom they clash."[15] The feminist movement is no exception to this rule. The ideology has been developed and disseminated by the relatively well-to-do. This is not to argue that active feminists are as well off as men, for this is surely not the case. Rather, when compared to women in general, those most sympathetic with the goal of equality tend to be of higher status.

Female scholars, active in support of feminism, have noted the class bias of the movement, some with dismay and others with sympathy. Margaret Mead, for example, is said to have infuriated some feminists when she described women's liberation as "essentially a middle class movement" spurred by "career drive." Similarly, Cynthia Epstein calls attention to the unrepresentative nature of women's organizations. She alleges that the National Organization for Women suffers a "stigma" because its membership is thought to be drawn disproportionately from "unmarried women." (It may still be true that success for women is measured by their ability to attract and keep a husband, hence being unmarried is more of a disgrace than it is for men.) If the "typical" woman is married, then the feminist movement may be especially sensitive about lack of accurate representation. The Sierra Club is not especially bothered by charges that it speaks for the wealthy, nor is Common Cause, or any of the liberal or progressive organizations. For women, however, there is a hint of disapproval in the implication that feminist ideology is a compensation for other failures. As Cynthia Epstein recalls, ". . . I attended the first Congress of United Women, a meeting in New York City of some 15 groups of women dedicated to 'women's liberation' and attended by about 300 participants. About 80 percent of the women—men were excluded—seemed to be college students or college graduates, under 30, single, interested in professional careers, and to the political left."[16]

The tone of this lament is consistent with our earlier discussion of the latent threat of feminism: *its implied wish to alter traditional male-female family roles.* It is certainly the case that opponents of feminist ideology, especially those women active in opposition to the Equal Rights Amendment, have focused their propaganda upon real or imagined threats to the family. And feminists themselves concede that the threat is ever present. The "ladies in pink" have made much of the fact that they are "typical" and that the feminists are not; that they are more involved with the nuclear family while their opponents are not. If feminism "seeks a redefinition of feminity and masculinity to denote not what men and women are expected to be but what they are capable of becoming when freed from the traditional sex linked roles which limit their potential for full emotional and intellectual development," and if it "critically examined existing patterns of social order, such as monogamous marriage, the nuclear family, and the capitalistic structure of the economy and proposes radical alternatives" small wonder that it is not attractive to average women.[17] In a single swoop, the feminist movement is said to challenge the economic system, the family system, and the political system. A more comprehensive program for the alienation of the masses can hardly be imagined.

Whether or not most active feminists believe that their goals can only be achieved by such radical changes is beside the point. Feminism does threaten established values, probably more than the earlier civil rights movement did. Black equality does not require a change in roles within families; its more modest goal is for equal participation in the political and economic system, rather than an alteration of that system. Although it is true that these goals have met white resistance, and more extreme groups never tire of raising the specter of interracial sex and marriage as the inevitable outcome of the civil rights movement, to grant blacks equality does not require much liberation from traditional roles.

Thus feminism is most attractive to those least bound by tradition—more educated women. Education is generally a liberating factor. It is almost a routine finding in survey research that education and tolerance are strongly related. The more educated are more tolerant of deviant opinions and life-styles. The less educated are more suspicious of change. The CBS/*New York Times* poll alluded to earlier, which found that 42 percent of the women interviewed felt the women's movement had been a major cause of family breakdown, also found that only 29 percent of women college graduates felt this way. Education and liberalism are strongly related. Research on women's values has repeatedly found that education is the key to acceptance of feminist ideology. Yankelovich pointed to a substantial disparity in the views of college and non-college women on a wide variety of social issues concerning the roles of women and men. Noting the more liberal and nontraditional values of college women, Yankelovich concluded that, to the extent that college women champion the causes of women's liberation, they are "inadvertently pulling many of the social underpinnings out from under young women who work because they need the money and who feel that their value in society is based on being good wives and mothers.[18]

There are numerous analogs to this sort of class (or educational) division. The "youth movement" of the late 1960s was nothing of the kind. While college-educated youths flocked to the banner of George McGovern and symbolic leaders of the New Left, their working class counterparts found George Wallace more to their liking. Early descriptions of the feminist movement reached similar conclusions. Jo Freeman, arguing that those who subscribed to *Ms.* magazine were "supporting" feminists, found that subscribers were highly educated, employed, yet earning considerably less money than their husbands. Obviously, supporting feminists were not typical women. They were more educated and more receptive to change. From a somewhat more hostile perspective, Jeane Kirkpatrick, using a 1972 Virginia Slims survey, concluded that approximately half of all women were hostile to feminist ideology and were "contented with their lot."[19]

Both Freeman and Kirkpatrick raise our expectations about the conditions for acceptance of feminist ideology. Freeman implies (and later in her books says explicitly) that well-educated women are attracted to feminism because of relative deprivation (they make less than their male counterparts); Kirkpatrick offers the same reasoning. If women were contented, then presumably they would have no need for an ideology so explicitly based upon change.

It would be genuinely astonishing if feminism were equally attractive to all women, regardless of education. A recent Gallup pool revealed that only approximately one-third of women interviewed believed they were "better off" in the past. Of this one-third, 57 percent of college graduates, 42 percent of high school graduates, and 39 percent of women who had only a grade school education believed that the women's movement had done a "great deal" to achieve such improvement. Our measure of the acceptance of feminism, the seven point scale, provides a more precise assessment of variance by education.

The responses shown in Table 1.1 strongly support the position that educated women are more sympathetic to feminism. (More

TABLE 1.1
Attitudes toward an Equal Role for Women Among Housewives and Employed Women, by Education (Percent Most Egalitarian)

	Employed Women			Housewives		
	High school	Some college	College	High school	Some college	College
1972	32	42	49	23	30	41
1974	33	46	55	18	37	29
1976	29	48	53	21	31	31
1978	44	53	64	24	26	41
1980	28	51	59	22	42	42
1982	45	43	58	26	35	38

detailed data are shown in Appendix B.) In 1972, employed women with some college or with a college degree were substantially more inclined toward the extreme egalitarian scale position. They were more feminist than their less educated counterparts in the workforce, more feminist than women with comparable education who were not in the workforce, and more feminist than men with comparable education. On the other hand, among those women who were housewives in 1972, there was a pronounced inclination to embrace the most traditional position. Fully 34 percent of the high school or lesser educated housewives chose the most traditional position. However, by 1982, the lesser educated housewives had moderated their traditionalist orientation significantly. What is striking is the across-the-board decline in traditionalist sentiment. By 1982, the support for the extreme traditionalist position had fallen below 10 percent for all groups except the lesser educated housewives and men. The more educated groups of employed women, who never showed much affection for extreme traditionalism, had reduced their responses to a mere chemical trace.

By using these two variables simultaneously, at least a partial understanding of the relative impact of employment experience and educational experience can be achieved. Education appears to have a greater impact upon the attitudes of women toward equality than men.[20] For example, as education increases within any year, the gap of support for extreme and moderate egalitarianism between employed women and men tends to increase. That is, education produces a more rapid increase in support for egalitarianism among employed women than it does for men. The same substantial impact of education can also be observed among housewives. Although few of them are college educated, and hence we cannot be more than tentative, education apparently contributes to feminism more for housewives than for men. This impact is especially apparent in recent years.

It has become commonplace to argue that men (especially younger men) are more feminist than women. By slight margins, men have been found, for example, to be more supportive of the Equal Rights Amendment. *Controlling for variables other than work experience,* the differences between men and women are usually not very large on equal rights/equal role/equal responsibility questions. Employed women, however, are more favorable to feminism than men, and men are more favorable to feminism than housewives (see Appendix B). Furthermore, *this holds generally for all levels of education.* Without a doubt, the key is work experience.

The sheer complexity of the interaction of work and education upon attitudes toward equality should refute the idea that women are a group. Furthermore, the complex interaction challenges stereotyped ideas of feminists as upper class, over-educated women with time on their hands. These ideas are simply not accurate. Once a woman enters the workforce, her attitudes change. However, as an *increasing percentage* of women are drawn into the workforce (an overwhelming percentage work out of necessity), these attitude changes are bound to affect American politics and society—because women will become more like a group.

While working class women (as measured by education) are indeed less feminist, perhaps too much has been made of this, and not enough attention paid to attitude change through time. Table 1.1 shows that the percentages of high school or less educated employed women and college-educated employed women on the egalitarian side of the scale have increased at roughly the same rate. Conversely, the percentages on the traditional side of the scale have decreased at about the same rate. In short, although lesser educated employed women are less supportive of equal rights, the gap between them and the college educated *has not increased. Support in both groups is increasing at roughly the same rate.*[21]

The assumptions about lower class women being less feminist are based to a considerable degree upon two phenomena. First, there is the well-established resistance of the less educated to social change, irrespective of its source and goals. Second, there is the problem of relative deprivation. If the lower class "knows its place," there should be "little distance between the rights a lower-class woman has and the rights she feels entitled to" according to Freeman.[22] Similarly, Carden argues that "middle and upper class college graduates are likely to feel the ensuing conflicts (e.g., between traditional female roles and the desire for professional accomplishment) most accutely. ..." Carden is pessimistic about the possibility of change, since she links the hostility of lower class women to the structure of the political and economic system. "It is reasonable that lower middle class and working class women should not be attracted to the new feminism and should, therefore, not even belong to the pool of potential recruits . . . a girl's peer group, parents, and counselors rarely urge her to prepare herself for any job more skilled than that of a secretary or beautician. Unlikely to go to college, she is, therefore, unlikely to be exposed to the alternative view points available there."[23] Similarly, Kathleen McCourt concludes that working class women "on the whole . . . view the feminist movement as of only limited value. It is perceived as relevant in some ways to unmarried women who have to support themselves and perhaps valuable for what it is doing in terms of guaranteeing equal pay for equal work. But certainly the women who are active in their communities do not in any way see their activity as part of a quest for personal liberation."[24]

We will look at the problem of relative deprivation in more depth later in the chapter. However, these points seem overstated. If we consider the data in any year, Freeman, Carden, and McCourt are quite correct. Employed women with the lowest education are indeed well behind the more educated cohorts: but, if one looks at the data over time, the gap is not increasing. To repeat in a different way the point made above, *a rising tide raises all boats*.

SUPPORT FOR THE WOMEN'S LIBERATION MOVEMENT

So far we have been discussing abstract ideology without reference to organizational efforts to implement the ideology. Women, depending upon their education and employment status, are more or less attracted or repelled by the notion of equality. This is not to say they are in sympathy with the strategy and tactics of various components of what is now known as the women's movement.

Acceptance of feminist ideology, but repudiation of feminist organizations, seems unlikely, but there is a fair amount of popular attention given to the possibility that the "average" woman resents the feminist superstars who jet about without concern for money, children, and numerous daily cares which plague the rest of us: "I'm all for women's lib, but . . . ." There is some truth to this idea, but not a great deal.

Beginning in 1970, respondents in the Survey Research Center's national election studies were asked to place themselves on a "feeling thermometer" (a 0° to 100° scale, ranging from very cold and unfavorable to very warm and favorable) when given the interview stimulus of "women's liberation movement" (which encompasses a variety of groups and individuals). Table 1.2 displays the relatively healthy correlations between the seven-point equal-role scale and the thermometer. The magnitude of the correlations increases significantly from 1972 to 1974 and then drops off through 1980. Only employed women remain relatively stable at a high level after 1974. Given the magnitude of the correlations, there clearly is some distinction being made between goals and organizations to implement the goals. However, it is not a major distinction.

Table 1.3 shows the mean of the feeling thermometer scores for the 1970-1980 period. When the question was first asked in 1970, most people were not favorably disposed toward women's liberation, to say the least. The highest thermometer reading, a decidedly chilly 36 degrees, was registered by employed women. By 1974, however, the scores had increased dramatically. Employed women registered

TABLE 1.2

Correlations between the Equal-Role Scale and the Women's Liberation Movement Feeling Thermometer

	1972	1974	1976	1980
Men	−.28	−.48	−.39	−.37
Employed women	−.32	−.48	−.44	−.46
Housewives	−.29	−.48	−.44	−.35

TABLE 1.3
Mean Feeling Thermometer Scores 1970-1980:

	Cross-Sectional Survey				
	1970	1972	1974	1976	1980
Men	34.8	46.2	52.9	51.9	53.3
Employed women	35.7	47.9	54.5	55.3	55.2
Housewives	28.8	42.2	49.8	49.6	52.8
	Panel Study				
		1972	1974	1976	
Men		46.9	53.8	53.1	
Employed women		48.0	53.4	54.8	
Housewives		39.2	50.1	49.8	

a 19 degree gain, housewives a 21 degree gain, and men an 18 degree gain. After 1974, the rate of increase fell off to nearly zero in both the cross-sectional and panel data. The largest increase between 1974 and 1980 was a three degree gain for housewives.

What is interesting about Table 1.3 is the apparent closeness of the three groups. The pattern we found in the equal role question is duplicated. Employed women are always more favorable to the women's liberation movement than men, and men are more favorable than housewives. By 1980, however, the gap among the three groups was less than three degrees.

These gaps become more significant when the education variable is added. Education has a strong impact upon the feelings about the women's liberation movement by employed women, some impact upon housewives, and *none* upon men (see Table 1.4). Although scores have increased for men, they have done so *uniformly*. Education seems to have little impact upon how men feel about women's organizations. In sharp contrast, college-educated employed women score significantly higher than lesser educated employed women. In fact, the 1980 results suggest that, unlike what we found for the equal role measure, the gap may be widening

TABLE 1.4
Mean Feeling Thermometer Scores 1970-1980, by Education

	High school					Some college					College				
	1970	1972	1974	1976	1980	1970	1972	1974	1976	1980	1970	1972	1974	1976	1980
Men	34.1	46.5	53.5	51.9	52.8	36.7	45.7	49.4	51.5	53.7	36.1	46.2	53.8	52.1	54.2
Employed women	36.5	44.9	52.7	53.6	49.8	33.9	47.8	55.9	57.6	58.6	36.6	57.6	59.6	58.6	65.8
Housewives	28.0	41.2	48.1	49.3	51.1	29.0	41.8	56.9	50.2	56.7	38.1	50.8	51.6	50.8	60.0

between the highly educated and the lesser educated employed women.

The magnitude of the correlations in Table 1.2, though substantial, are such that they allow a "half-full/half-empty glass" type of analysis. Clearly, support for abstract ideology and support for a group or groups championing the ideology are not the same thing. Both measures show support, increasingly rapidly through 1974 and then leveling off. Both are still increasing, but at a very slow rate. The tailing off in the correlations, especially for men and housewives, indicates that the antifeminist movement, which, as we discussed above, emerged as a significant political force between 1972-1974, may have had a greater impact upon men generally and women who were not in the labor force.

Work sharply increases a woman's support for the idea of equality, but not necessarily for organizations that champion it. Receptivity to these organizations is closely tied to the employed woman's education. It is the lesser educated employed women, then, who conform closely to the stereotype "I'm all for women's lib but. . . ."

Although housewives were the least receptive group both to the idea of equality and to the organizations pushing it, they significantly increased their support for both in the decade of the seventies. Education has a clear impact upon a housewife's feelings about the women's liberation movement. Although housewives trail employed women in every respect, education has a similar impact upon their attitudes.

Men appear to want their cake and eat it too. Men, especially the highly educated as of 1982, strongly support equality. However, they don't appear to be crazy about the women's liberation movement. Numerous surveys have shown that in families where both spouses are employed, the woman is still saddled with most of the domestic work. Men apparently feel it's great that women get equal pay (in this age of inflation the money helps), but when it comes to the home, they don't want to do the work their mothers did. However, this is bound to change. Women now make up over half the enrollment in U.S. colleges and universities. As more women attain higher levels of education and enter the labor force, support for women's organizations and goals will continue to increase. This in turn, will inevitably affect the division of labor in the home.

LIFE SATISFACTION AND WORK

Is work good for you? More specifically, does employment make you more satisfied? This is not an idle question. For years, men have been assumed to derive most life satisfaction from work; women were presumed to derive most life satisfaction from the home. Men are said to be "married to their jobs." Such an allegation applies only to those men whose jobs are not routine—professionals. But what about women? As the labor force becomes populated by women (less so at professional levels), do they become married to their jobs? Or do they feel more tension between home and work, a lingering ambivalence related to traditional gender roles?

Dissatisfaction is assumed to be the dynamo of protest groups. Otherwise, why protest? The violence and tension associated with the black civil rights movement assumed (rightly) that blacks were more dissatisfied with their personal lives than were whites. It is easy to aggregate blacks, as a group, and to describe their high level of personal dissatisfaction. For women, we encounter the same complexity that we encountered in discussing their commitment to feminism. Although popular stereotypes assume that women are either dissatisfied (from the point of view of feminist leaders) or happy (from the point of view of extreme traditionalists), both sides are wrong.

It is true, as revealed by most popular surveys, that women are as happy as men. In 1979, for example, exactly 77 percent of both women and men indicated satisfaction with "the way things are going in your own personal life."[25] Such similarities are neither new nor surprising. Virtually identical results can be found in every major survey of women and men. Both sexes, as long as they are white, report virtually identical satisfaction with standards of living, work, family income, and the future. If times are hard, pessimism afflicts both sexes equally. If times are good, optimism rises equally.

Are women lying? Are they afraid to tell interviewers the real truth about their oppression? Or do they fail to understand the dimensions of oppression? The latter argument is more plausible, and more satisfying to feminist leaders. In an economic and political world dominated by men, the general level of satisfaction on the part of women may be due to their inability to recognize and respond to discrimination. "False consciousness," the inability to comprehend the nature of oppression, argues that even if women are reporting their level of satisfaction honestly, they are "lying" to themselves in that they are inaccurate in their perceptions. They fail to understand the extent to which they are locked into the acceptance of inferior status by institutions and tradition. The "lie" itself is, therefore, significant. In the early phases of the feminist movement, small consciousness raising sessions were undertaken in order to eliminate false consciousness. Although such groups are no longer as active as they once were, it is significant that they were undertaken at all. Blacks did not engage in consciousness raising; but their consciousness was raised. As a consequence of the civil rights movement, the proportion of blacks using race as a personal frame of reference for individual identification increased substantially. On the other hand, a form of consciousness raising was used in various socialist revolutions; groups of workers were lectured about the necessity of revolution. In fact, Lenin's belief in the vanguard of the revolution tacitly assumed that there would be, at least initially, little support among the intended beneficiaries, the workers.

For women, the source of false consciousness is not the economic system, but the family. The centrality of the family in the lives of both men and women lends credence to the notion that the family operates to the disadvantage of women. It is through the family that roles are initially established, and authority patterns developed. The employed women of today feel more tension between job and family than do men. This is the case because, irrespective of their protestations of equality, men do not share equally in household tasks when both parents are employed. Employed women with children also retain the bulk of the responsibility and drudgery of running a house (men are especially averse to changing diapers). There is more tension involved when mothers are employed; there is strong support for employed mothers, yet a fear that the children will suffer.

To the extent that changing the status quo involves changing the family, or altering the division of responsibility within the family, the changes are threatening to both men and women. Even if the status quo is changed because of economic necessity, the threat is there: "feminism need not formulate radical programs aimed toward the alteration of family life in order to appear threatening to the family; laying bare familiar sex conflicts is threatening in and of itself."[26] Perhaps sex conflict is potentially so severe and damaging that it must consciously or unconsciously be abjured by both sexes.

Housewives, who should be miserable, deny that this is the case. In 1968, 1972, and 1976, respondents were asked the question: "In general, how satisfying do you find the way you're spending your life these days? Would you call it completely satisfying, pretty satisfying, or not very satisfying?" If we compare the answers for the three years (see Table 1.5), employed women had the lowest percentage in the completely satisfied category and the highest percentage in the not very satisfied category in each year. Although the gaps are narrowing, employed women are least satisfied and housewives are most satisfied.

Let us acknowledge that housewives may be victims of false consciousness. Indeed, there is some evidence that this is the case, based upon less obtrusive indicators of dissatisfaction; more mood-altering drugs are prescribed for housewives than for employed women or men. Housewives are more likely (but only slightly) to seek professional counseling. On the other hand, employed men have a higher rate of heart attacks, ulcers, and other stress-related illnesses than do either employed women or housewives, and there is more alcoholism among employed men than there is among

TABLE 1.5
Satisfaction with Life

	Men	Employed women	Housewives
	1968		
Completely	23.3*	20.5	26.5
Pretty	67.5	68.9	64.1
Not very	9.1	10.9	9.3
	1972		
Completely	21.8	18.4	26.0
Pretty	68.3	70.5	65.8
Not very	9.8	11.1	8.2
	1976		
Completely	18.6	16.7	21.1
Pretty	71.4	70.2	68.1
Not very	10.0	13.0	10.8

*All entries are percentages.

housewives or employed women. In any case, it may be true that the happiness of housewives conceals a more serious pathology, but it probably is not.

More important for our purposes is the verification of the notion of feminism being most attractive to those who need it most, those who have presumably personal experience with discrimination: employed women. Just as employed women are more attracted to feminism, so are they less personally satisfied. Employed women are subject to more strain; the deprivations of sex discrimination are more *relatively* severe since they have a readily identified group from which to draw comparisons. Thus, more relatively deprived, they are more in need of an organization and ideology which does not rationalize their inferior status but which does demand more equality.

This phenomenon—the relationship between dissatisfaction and feminism—is crucial to the understanding of the dynamics of protest. Employed women should become more feminist as they become more dissatisfied. In 1972, satisfaction was clearly linked to feminism for employed women (see Table 1.6). As satisfaction decreases, the thermometer score rises and the person is found closer to the equal-role end of the seven-point scale. Ironically, in 1972, satisfaction and attitudes toward feminist organizations appeared to be linked, for both men and housewives. For housewives the effect was weak, but for men it was not. However, men's attitudes toward equality appeared not to be linked to satisfaction, while housewives' attitudes appeared to be toward equality. We have previously noted that people make a distinction between feminist ideology and feminist organizations—this is merely one more example of the complexity of this phenomenon.

By 1976, the link between feminism and satisfaction had disappeared for housewives, was unclear for men, but was still present—though considerably weaker—for employed women. Interestingly, unlike 1972, unhappy men in 1976 were located significantly closer to the equal-role end of the seven-point scale than their happy counterparts. The values for employed women are less significant because they are already so close to the equal-role end that little movement is possible. In any case, dissatisfied employed women's attraction to feminist organizations is clear.

Perhaps some of the dissatisfaction (and perhaps some of the attraction to abstract equality) may be due to the fact that employed

TABLE 1.6
Satisfaction with Life by Thermometer Score and Position on the Equal-Role Scale

	1972						1976					
	Men		Employed women		Housewives		Men		Employed women		Housewives	
	Therm	Equal role	Therm	Equal role	Therm	Equal role	Therm	Equal role	Therm	Equal role	Therm	Equal role
Completely	42.5	3.4	42.1	3.5	40.9	4.0	52.9	3.0	54.2	2.6	45.6	4.0
Pretty	46.3	3.4	48.5	3.0	42.3	4.1	50.8	3.1	55.1	2.9	51.6	3.8
Not very	51.8	3.5	53.4	2.9	44.1	3.5	58.6	2.4	58.7	2.4	45.7	4.0

women have two jobs—household maintenance and their outside work—whereas housewives and men really have only one. Additionally, ambivalence on the part of employed women, an ambivalence based upon traditional roles, may be at work. Attachment to children, and the belief that a working mother damages her children, is enough guilt to make anyone feel bad. The attachment of women to children is not women's sole biological destiny, but it is nonetheless real.[27]

To explore the idea that employment and maintaining a household make married women dissatisfied, we can examine the responses of employed women who are married in comparison to those who are not. Both, of course, may have children, especially if the single women are divorced.

Married and single women appear to be quite different (see Table 1.7). In 1972, personal satisfaction and feminism were more strongly related for married employed women than for single employed women. However, by 1976, the relationship vanished for married employed women, but was still very strong for single employed women.

As a group, married employed women strongly support an equal role for themselves and feel very positive toward the women's liberation movement. By 1976, this support for feminism appeared to be unrelated to how they felt about their personal lives. Marriage has emotional rewards unrelated to one's employment. Evidently, these rewards are greater than the strains produced by the unequal division of labor in the home.

In general, married people are happier than single people. Only about six percent of married employed women in both 1972 and 1976 said they were unhappy, compared with 18 and 23 percent of

TABLE 1.7

Satisfaction with Life by Thermometer Score and Equal-Role Positions for Single and Married Employed Women

	1972				1976			
	Married		Single		Married		Single	
Completely	41.7	3.3	43.0	4.1	54.9	2.7	52.5	2.4
Pretty	47.8	3.0	49.5	2.7	54.2	3.0	56.6	2.8
Not very	58.3	2.8	51.0	3.1	50.9	2.5	61.8	2.5

single women. (For men the figures were 7 and 18 percent.) In 1980, single employed women felt the warmest of any group toward women's liberation and had the highest level of support for an equal role with men. In sum, single employed women (and most especially, *unhappy* single employed women) are the ideal group to be recruited by feminist organizations.

FEMINISM: DIFFUSION, AWARENESS, AND CONSTRAINT

The data that we have examined so far have a common thread running through them. Support for feminism and feminist organizations increased steeply in the early 1970s, leveled off around 1974, and has increased very slowly, if at all, since. Why is this the case? Why hasn't feminism been more successful? The obvious answer, which we have already briefly discussed, is the emergence during 1972-74 of a strong grassroots anti-ERA movement, led by Phyllis Schlafly. What we wish to do in the remainder of this chapter is to put this obvious answer in an explicit theoretical context so that we may better understand the dynamics of attitudinal change in the decade of the seventies. To do this, we need to know something about diffusion, awareness, and constraint.

According to Philip Converse, as an ideology moves beyond the "miniscale proportion responsible for 'creative synthesis,' it tends to 'be diffused in "packages,"' which consumers come to see as 'natural' wholes...."[28] Such a "package" is more or less *constrained*—that is, it is more or less possible to predict one's attitude on one component part from knowledge of an attitude about another component part. Thus, "religion as the opiate of the masses" and "the exploitation of the working class by the capitalists" are linked together by classical Marxism. To know that a person is a Marxist and believes that religion is the opiate of the masses is to be able to predict with near certainty that he or she believes the proletariat is exploited by the capitalist class.

On a less abstract level, if we know a person is a liberal Democrat and is opposed to nuclear power, then we can reliably predict that the person is opposed to the use of phenoxy-herbicides, opposes the B1 bomber and the neutron bomb, favors more spending on food stamps, and so on.

But to know "what goes with what" does not necessarily require that a person know *why* the ideas and beliefs go together; a person can know that a set of ideas go together but not know the rationales for the conjunction. To use Converse's example, most Americans know that "communists are Godless," but very few know why. Furthermore, a person may become *aware* of these "packages," and the substance of an ideology of which they are a part, *without accepting them.* Converse's model suggests that diffusion can increase both awareness and constraint and that the former will increase more than the latter.

We developed a measure of awareness using a respondent's perceptions of the various candidates and groups' positions on the equal-role scale in 1972 to divide the respondents into two groups; those who were minimally aware of feminism and those who were not. (See Appendix A for details.) Unfortunately, we could not perform the same analysis on the equal-role scale in 1976—which would have allowed us to measure directly the change in awareness over the period—because the response task in 1976 was quite different. The only stimuli in common in the two years were the two major political parties.

We will apply the technique to the panel study because diffusion is an inherently time related process and is best investigated by looking at the same respondents over time. By dividing the three gender groups in the panel study into aware and unaware subgroups, we should be able to study diffusion directly.

If the model is correct, those who were aware in 1972 should have more stable opinions over the four-year period than the unaware. The aware groups should also have higher levels of constraint. Finally, because of the controversies surrounding the Equal Rights Amendment, abortion, and affirmative action, which began in earnest in the early 1970s, awareness certainly increased. Accordingly, "doorstep opinions" probably decreased. This should be manifested in a narrowing of the gaps between aware and unaware groups when other confounding variables (e.g., education) are controlled for.

In addition to the equal-role scale and the women's liberation movement feeling thermometer, we will be analyzing the responses to five attitude questions concerning the role of women in the home and the workplace in this section. These questions tap both attitudes toward equality and attitudes about the usefulness of women's organization. Unfortunately, this group of questions was asked only in 1972 and 1976, which limits their utility for earlier sections of this chapter. However, in this context, the number of profeminist responses to these questions should provide a useful check on the responses to the thermometer and equal role scale. (See Appendix B for quesion wording and coding.)

Overall, 16 percent of the housewives, 30 percent of the employed women, and 36 percent of the men locating themselves on the equal-role scale in all three years of the panel study were aware. Table 1.8 shows the results for the six subgroups on the equal-role scale. (Appendix B shows a more detailed set of tables.)

Awareness has a big impact upon employed women and housewives but little impact upon men. The distribution of aware and unaware men is very similar in all three years of the panel study. The difference between their mean thermometer scores is very small and does not even approach statistical, let alone substantive, significance. Although almost 10 percent more men in the aware group gave profeminist responses to the attitude questions, this percentage is smaller than the gap between aware and unaware employed women and aware and unaware housewives (approximately 17 and 13 percent, respectively).

Among the unaware, housewives trailed employed women and men on all the measures. Among the aware, employed women showed the highest levels of support on all the measures, followed by housewives, who in turn were clearly more supportive than men.

Our hypothesis that the gaps between the aware and unaware should narrow from 1972 to 1976 is for the most part correct. The distribution of aware and unaware employed women over the equal-role scale are clearly more similar by 1976. The gap between the

TABLE 1.8

Relationship between Awareness and Preference for an Equal Role for Women (Percent Most Egalitarian)

	Employed		Housewives	
	Aware	Unaware	Aware	Unaware
1972	51	33	43	22
1974	49	39	52	24
1976	40	30	39	26

feeling thermometer means also decreases, but the gap on the attitude questions actually increased one percent. Similarly, the gap between aware and unaware housewives remained essentially unchanged on the attitude questions, decreased on the thermometer, and increased on the equal-role scale. For men the gaps, although never large, decrease on all three measures. In sum, support for feminism increased between 1972 and 1976 in all subgroups with the rate of increase being slightly greater for the unaware.

Breaking down Table 1.8 by education produces few surprises. Generally speaking, support for feminism increases within each subgroup by education. The gaps, however, do not follow a clear-cut pattern because the N's (number of cases) get so small among the aware. However, there is tendency for the gaps to reduce at a more rapid rate among the highly educated.

Our hypothesis that the unaware groups should have lower levels of constraint is strongly supported by the data. To measure constraint, we computed the correlations between the equal-role scale, the feeling thermometer, and the number of profeminist responses to the five attitude questions. This produces three correlation values. We then computed the mean of the absolute values of the three correlations to arrive at an overall measure. The results, broken down by education and awareness, are displayed in Table 1.9.

Considering first the total columns within each gender category, the level of constraint was, without exception, higher for the aware subgroup. However, the increase in constraint from 1972 to 1976 was highest for the unaware groups, thereby narrowing the gap between the aware and unaware. The largest gain in constraint was registered by the unaware housewives, followed by unaware employed women and unaware men. For the aware group as a whole, disregarding gender, the mean constraint value was the same in 1972 and 1976 (.50). Table 1.9 shows that constraint actually increased for employed women, decreased for housewives, and remained nearly the same for men, thus producing no overall net change.

The relationship between education and constraint is uneven. However, except for aware housewives and unaware employed women, the high school educated within each subgroup had a lower constraint value than the college educated. For aware housewives and unaware employed women in 1976, the relationship between

TABLE 1.9
Constraint by Awareness, Education, and Sex

		Aware				Unaware			
		High school	Some college	College	Total	High school	Some college	College	Total
Men	1972	.34[a]	.57	.43	.44	.23	.33	.42	.29
	1976	.28	.51	.47	.43	.34	.30	.64	.34
	N	44	56	61	161	129	99	36	264
Employed women	1972	.47	.51	.65	.55	.35	.39	.26	.37
	1976	.45	.63	.62	.59	.45	.44	.37	.44
	N	15	34	26	75	80	54	22	156
Housewives	1972	.63	.51	.54	.58	.37	.47	.38	.41
	1976	.68	.39	.31	.53	.47	.55	.65	.51
	N	21	10	11	42	122	44	20	186

[a] Mean of absolute values of the correlations between the seven point scale, the five attitude questions, and the thermometer.

constraint and education was actually negative—as education increased, constraint decreased. In the case of the housewives, this inverse relationship has to be interpreted with caution due to the small N's (21, 10, and 11, respectively). Although counterintuitive, the inverse relationship for employed women also cannot bear much interpretational weight because the spread of the mean values, .08, is small.

Our hypothesis that the aware groups should have more stable opinions than the unaware groups is also supported by the data. The percentage of responses remaining stable (either pro/pro or anti/anti) is highest for the aware subgroup in each gender group. This result holds when education is controlled as well. We also cross-tabulated the 1972, 1974, and 1976 equal-role scales and found that, no matter which pair of years is chosen, the percentage of aware respondents remaining at the same point on the scale is higher than the corresponding unaware respondents for each gender group.

Interestingly, taken together men were much more volatile (i.e., changing their positions more from year to year) on all three measures of support than women. This is certainly implied by the fact that men, both aware and unaware, had the lowest levels of constraint in both 1972 and 1976. For example, 28 percent of employed women and 32 percent of housewives located themselves at the same position on the equal-role scale in all three years, while only 23 percent of men did so. If people in each group that changed consistently—that is, became either monotonically less or more feminist—are added in, then the percentages become 81, 75, and 66 respectively.[29]

In conclusion, our hypothesis regarding how stability of opinion and constraint are affected by awareness is strongly confirmed. Our hypothesis that because awareness almost certainly increased between 1972 and 1976, the attitudinal gaps between the aware and unaware (as defined in 1972) should narrow is less strongly confirmed. This bears some further examination.

It is easy to see from the N's in Table 1.9 that high-school educated or lesser educated people are overrepresented among the unaware and underrepresented among the aware. Approximately 52 percent of unaware men and employed women and 71 percent of housewives were in the high school or less category. The corresponding figures for the aware gender groups are 22, 28, and 50 percent, respectively. Consequently, because support for feminism varies with education, even if both aware groups were equally aware the "unaware" group would lag behind the "aware" in its support (i.e., if one doesn't control for education). Now, as we discussed above, constraint increased significantly among the unaware but not the aware. This in turn implies that there was a significant gain in awareness on the part of the unaware because awareness is a necessary (but not sufficient) condition for constraint to occur. Finally, the attitudinal gaps between the aware and unaware, regardless of gender category, do decrease at a more rapid rate among the college educated.

What does all this mean? Clearly, the college-educated panel respondents who were not very informed in 1972 picked up information about these issues and formed more consistent opinions at a much more rapid rate than their high-school educated counterparts. By 1976, the attitudinal distributions of the college-educated aware and unaware groups within each gender category were much more alike than the corresponding lesser-educated groups. This implies that the rate of *horizontal diffusion* (i.e., the acceptance of an ideology by more members of the same social class as the movement's leaders) was greater than the rate of *vertical diffusion* (i.e., the acceptance of an ideology by members of other, usually lower, social classes).

There is no escaping the conclusion that a considerable degree of diffusion took place. But diffusion does not necessarily result in the dissemination of the original "pure" ideology. As social movements mature, they frequently modify their demands to adjust to estimates of the probability of success. Yesterday's extremists become today's moderates.[30] Additionally, just as organization breeds counter-organization, competing ideologies will emerge. In some cases, competing ideologies do not appeal to the same social classes as the original protest movements do; in other cases, they appeal to the same constituency. In either case, changes in the original ideology usually results.

Phyllis Schlafly's activities from 1972 onward clearly fit into our model. Before 1972, Schlafly (the author of *A Choice not an Echo,* a book promoting Barry Goldwater's 1964 presidential candidacy) was not widely known outside of Republican conservative circles. In late 1972, she began her campaign to prevent ratification of the Equal Rights Amendment. Through the use of her newsletter, *The Eagle Forum Organization,* and the STOP-ERA organization, she became nationally known by mid-1974. She subsequently expanded her activities to include opposition to abortion, which she views as closely tied to the Equal Rights Amendment, and opposition to any revision of the Social Security system that would change the present method of dependent's benefits; she regards such revisions as antifamily, a "plan to drive all wives and mothers out of the home and into the workforce."[31] Schlafly is now one of the leaders of not simply an anti-ERA or an antiabortion movement, but a true antifeminist movement.

The strength of this antifeminist movement has its limits. Although support for feminism did level off in the mid-1970s, it still continues to increase and shows every sign that the rate of increase, though small, will continue. Demographics are clearly on the side of the feminist movement. More women are getting more education, more women are employed, and fewer are staying in the home. Furthermore, there are many signs of moderation in the feminist movement—a clear sign that it is a mature and lasting social movement. To cite just one example, Betty Friedan, in her book *The Second Stage,* argues that feminists need to pay closer attention to the family.

This maturation/moderation raises another question: Are we approaching the high tide of feminist success? Were the seventies the period of rapid gains, and are the eighties to be the period of consolidation? We will attempt to answer these questions in later chapters.

NOTES

1. Jo Freeman, "The Women's Liberation Movement: Its Origins, Structures, Impact, and Ideas," in Freeman, Ed., *Women: A Feminist Perspective* (Palo Alto, Calif.: Mayfield, 1975), p. 448.

2. Maren L. Carden, *The New Feminist Movement* (New York: Russell Sage, 1974), p. 153; see also June Sochen, *Movers and Shakers: American Women Thinkers and Activists 1900-1970* (New York: Quadrangle, 1973), and Virginia Sapiro, *The Political Integration of Women* (Urbana, Ill.: University of Illinois Press, 1983), pp. 18-20.

3. Janet Boles, *The Politics of the Equal Rights Amendment* (New York: Longman, 1979), chap. 3.

4. Nora Glazer, "Sex and Sex Roles," in Glazer and Helen Waehrer, Ed., *Women in a Man Made World* (Chicago: Rand McNally, 1977), p. 255.

5. Judith Hole and Ellen Levine, *Rebirth of Feminism* (New York: Quadrangle, 1971), p. 200.

6. Two major works address this question. They are Virginia Sapiro, *The Political Integration of Women* (see note 2), and Claire Fulenwider, *Feminism in American Politics* (New York: Praeger, 1980).

7. "One study conducted by Thomas Juster of the Institute for Social Research at the University of Michigan found that men aged 25 to 44 spent an average

of 14.1 hours per week on housework and child care in 1981, up from 11.8 hours in 1965. Yet women of the same age, most of whom are now working outside the home, spent 31.8 hours on the job at home, down from 45.9 hours in 1965." Ann Crittenden, "We 'Liberated' Mothers Aren't," *Washington Post,* 5 February 1984, p. D1.

8. Virginia Sapiro, "News From the Front: Inter-Sex and Inter-Generational Conflict Over the Status of Women," paper presented at the 1977 annual meeting of the American Political Science Association, p. 1. A revised version of this paper was later published in the Western Political Quarterly 2 (June 1980): 260: 277.

9. Carden, *The New Feminist Movement,* p. 29.

10. The 1980 Virginia Slims American Women's Opinion Poll. A study conducted by the Roper Organization.

11. *New York Times,* 19 Aug. 1984, p. 6.

12. Sapiro, "News From the Front," pp.16-17.

13. U.S. Department of Commerce, Bureau of the Census, *A Statistical Portrait,* Current Population Reports, 58 (Washington, D.C.: U.S. Government Printing Office, 1980) p. 50.

14. See Eileen L. McDonagh, "To Work or Not To Work: The Differential Impact of Achieved and Derived Status upon the Political Participation of Women, 1956-1976," *American Journal of Political Science* 2 (May 1982): 280-297.

15. Anthony Oberschall, *Social Conflict and Social Movements* (Englewood Cliffs, N.J.: Prentice-Hall, 1973), p. 155.

16. Cynthia Epstein, *Woman's Place* (Berkeley: University of California Press, 1970), pp. 39-40.

17. Sapiro, "News From the Front," pp. 16-17.

18. Daniel Yankelovich, *The New Morality* (New York: McGraw-Hill, 1974), p. 116.

19. Freeman, *The Politics of Women's Liberation* (New York: Longman, 1975), p. 70, Jeane Kirkpatrick, *The New Presidential Elite* (New York: Russell Sage, 1976), p. 439.

20. Similar conclusions were reached by Sapiro, *The Political Integration of Women,* p. 76, and by Fulenwider, *Feminism in American Politics.* Fulenwider concludes: "Clearly the overall educational level of the population has not

changed measurably.... What appears to have changed is the level of acceptance of feminism, a change led by the better educated." (p. 61).

21. Again, employment contributes to feminism, irrespective of the motives for seeking it. See Myra Marx Ferree, "Working Class Feminism: A Consideration of the Consequences of Employment," *Sociological Quarterly 21* (Spring 1980), pp. 173-184.

22. Freeman, *The Politics of Women's Liberation*, p. 70.

23. Carden, *The New Feminist Movement*, pp. 140-141.

24. Kathleen McCourt, *Working Class Women and Grass Roots Politics* (Bloomington, Ind.: Indiana University Press, 1977), p. 183.

25. *Gallup Political Index,* March 1979, p. 3.

26. Sapiro, "News From the Front," pp. 16-17.

27. Women are more interested in, and more involved with, educational politics at the local level than they are with, for example, city politics. While the opportunities for participation are higher, so too is the identity of women with the education of the child. Women rarely advance administratively in education, but they make up approximately one-third of the membership of school boards. See M. Kent Jennings and Norman Thomas, "Men and Women in Party Elites: Social Roles and Political Resources," *Midwest Journal of Political Science 12* (November 1968), pp. 469-492.

28. Philip E. Converse, "The Nature of Belief Systems in Mass Publics," in David E. Apter, Ed., *Ideology and Discontent* (New York: Free Press, 1964), p. 211. See also Arland Thornton and Deborah Freedman, "Consistency of Sex Role Attitudes of Women, 1962-1974," University of Michigan Institute for Social Research, August 1979. Fulenwider, *Feminism in American Politics,* is the most explicit application of the various theories of constraint to women.

29. For example, a person who became monotonically less feminist would have a pattern such as 2-2-3 or 5-6-6 or 5-6-7, and so on.

30. See William A. Gamson, *The Strategy of Social Protest* (Homewood, Ill.: The Dorsey Press, 1975).

31. For Schlafly's views on abortion, see her *Eagle Forum* flyer, *The Abortion Connection.* For a more extensive discussion on her views of changes in the Social Security system, see *The Phyllis Schlafly Report,* June 1979.

2
Women and the Vote: An Overview of Recent Presidential Elections

Women have only been able to vote since 1920. To the modern reader, nurtured on media coverage of the civil rights movement, the idea that any portion of the adult population could be legally disqualified from voting appears to be the ultimate in repression. Yet women have been legally able to vote for a far shorter period of time than blacks. All of this is prefatory to the discussion of several aspects of women's voting behavior. For example, it is generally believed that women participate less than men and do not vote cohesively. There is some truth in these claims, but are they true of other recent entrants into the political process as well? When the voting age was lowered to 18, we soon learned that, contrary to the hopes of liberal Democrats and to the fears of conservative Republicans, "youth" voted less often and with less cohesion than did other, older, more established categoric groups.

There is every reason to assume that women will be no more or less active or cohesive than men. Their preferences will be determined less by the fact of gender than by other aspects of their lives—party affiliation, income, or ideology. Disappointment that women do not join together to repel antifeminist candidates is understandable when this disappointment is expressed by feminist leaders, but it neglects one fundamental aspect of women's political behavior, a point with which we began this book. Women are not a single bloc. Of all the groups available for analysis, only blacks appear to vote consistently and cohesively for Democratic candidates for president. Other portions of the Democratic coalition are fickle: Members of unions deserted the Democrats in 1972 and, to a lesser degree, in 1980. Mexican-Americans also found Reagan relatively attractive. All of these groups can legitimately claim to have been represented during the election. Blacks, working class whites, and Mexican-Americans surely are at least symbolically better off when Democrats win, since Democrats are the party of the working class, the "little man," and so forth. For women, no clear-cut distinction emerges. Not until 1972 was there even a contest in which one of the candidates appeared more in sympathy with women's issues. Even then, the ill-fated candidacy of George McGovern was not directed to any significant degree toward these issues. In 1976, both candidates were sufficiently adept at blurring their politics that everyone had trouble figuring out what they stood for. In 1980, of course, Ronald Reagan was opposed to the Equal Rights Amendment and to abortion. But, as we shall see, the election was hardly a referendum on these issues.

Women changed dramatically between 1967 and 1982. They entered the workforce in significant numbers. In 1980, 52 percent of all women were employed, comprising about 43 percent of the workforce. In our samples, 41 percent were employed in 1968, compared to 48 percent in 1982. Of more interest, however, is the fact that 49 percent claimed to be housewives in 1968 compared to only 27 percent in 1982. There are great changes here. For example, the increase in employed women is in excess of the decrease in the percentage who claim to be housewives; what happened to them? Probably they came to regard themselves as unemployed, or perhaps retired; in any case, many women no longer identified themselves as housewives.[1] Clearly, the diffusion of feminist ideas and beliefs profoundly affected women's perception of the word "housewife" in all its connotations.

A broad overview of voting preference and voting participation levels for women and men since 1968 both confirms and rejects the stereotypes. Consider the rate of participation. Women are less likely than men to vote, but the differences are hardly overwhelming (see Table 2.1). Most of the disparity can be explained by the fact that housewives don't vote as often as employed women. Since the housewife is becoming an endangered species, it is not surprising that differences between the rate of participation for men and women was not large in 1980. Employed women participated at the

TABLE 2.1
Participation in the 1980 Presidential Election, by Gender

	1980			
	Total men	Total women	Employed women	Housewives
Reagan	40.2[a]	33.3	36.2	34.1
Carter	26.0	29.6	29.5	26.9
Anderson	6.1	5.9	7.2	4.8
Not voting	27.7	31.2	27.1	34.1
n	592	766	376	208

[a]All entries are percentages. Columns may not sum to 100 percent of rounding error or minor party candidates.

same rate as did men in 1972 and in 1980; in the 1968 and 1976 elections they participated at a slightly lower rate.[2] So much for the idea that women are not interested in politics because public affairs are "best left to men."[3] Housewives do lag behind, but probably in a few more years there will be so few women willing to claim the title that it will cease to be a significant category.

The contours of the vote do not lend themselves to easy generalization (see Table 2.2). Women divided their vote between Humphrey and Nixon in 1968; disliked McGovern (as did everybody else) in 1972; divided their vote between Carter and Ford in 1976; and gave Reagan a slight nod in 1980.[4] If we argue that 1972 and 1980 were two elections in which at least the semblance of an ideological choice existed,* then women are more conservative than liberal in their preferences.

However, if we compare their behavior with that of men, we can consider another conclusion. It is true that they preferred Nixon to McGovern, but less so than men did. The two elections (1968 and 1976) in which their vote most closely approximated men's votes clearly emerged as less ideological ones. What was the difference between Nixon and Humphrey? Between Carter and Ford? Perhaps

*Setting aside the issue of viability, Wallace in 1968 clearly presented the voter with an ideological choice vis-à-vis Humphrey and Nixon, but he had no chance of winning.

TABLE 2.2
Distribution of Reported Voters by Gender for Four Presidential Elections

	Men	Women	Employed women	Housewives		Men	Women	Employed women	Housewives
	1968					*1972*			
Humphrey	40.1*	46.1	51.6	41.4	McGovern	32.0	43.5	43.5	30.3
Nixon	45.5	45.8	42.9	48.3	Nixon	68.0	61.4	56.5	69.8
Wallace	14.4	8.0	5.6	10.2					
	1976					*1980*			
Ford	48.9	48.5	46.9	54.0	Reagan	55.6	48.4	49.7	51.8
Carter	49.4	51.0	52.9	46.0	Carter	36.0	43.0	40.5	40.9
					Anderson	8.4	8.6	9.9	7.3

*All entries are percentages. Columns may not sum to 100 percent because of rounding error or minor party candidates.

a good summary is that women will pick conservatives over liberals, but less so than men do. Thus, while women gave Reagan a slight edge, men found him far more attractive than Carter.

Although much has been made of the differences between men and women in their 1980 voting (NOW calls it "Reagan's Female Problem"),[5] Table 2.2 reveals no clear *trend* in the difference between male and female voting behavior. In terms of major party candidates, the gap between women and men was about the same in 1980 as it was in 1972—7.1 percent versus 6.6 percent, respectively. In between these two elections, 1976, the gap all but disappeared.

The gaps between women and men in their congressional election voting also show no clear trend as of 1982. In 1982, women were 5 percent more favorable to Democratic candidates than were men. Though significant, this gap is smaller than those in 1966, 1962, and 1956, which were 9, 6, and 10 percent, respectively. In all three of those years, women were more favorable to the Republican congressional candidates.[6]

It is intriguing to compare the voting preferences of employed women with those of housewives. As we noted in Chapter 1, employed women find the ideology of feminism more acceptable than housewives do. They also find nominally liberal candidates more to their liking. In 1968 and 1972, they lent more support to the Democratic candidate than did housewives, and they also found Carter marginally more satisfying. But in 1980, this was not the case; Reagan pulled about the same percentage of votes from both employed women and housewives. Were employed women becoming more conservative or was the election truly a referendum on Jimmy Carter? It is an ironic tribute to Carter's lack of stature that, in spite of his opponent's blatantly antifeminist posturing, employed women (who accept feminism) supported Reagan to about the same extent as did housewives. Carter edged out Reagan (and Ford) only among that nebulous category we call "other women" (perhaps for a candidate who admitted to having "lust in his heart," the support of the "other woman" is welcome).

Breaking voting participation down by education reveals some interesting patterns. In 1968, education was strongly related to votes for Nixon, but not to votes for Humphrey. This holds for all categories. Far fewer women than men voted for Wallace, and as education increased, support for him among women decreased. Overall, women split their vote evenly between Nixon and

Humphrey. However, this disguises a significant difference between employed women and housewives; employed women went for Humphrey while housewives opted for Nixon.

The panel data with the awareness filter offers a splendid opportunity to dig beneath the surface in 1972 and 1976. The former, 1972, is especially valuable because the Democratic candidate, George McGovern, lent his name to the newly emergent women's movement and was actively supported by feminist leaders.

Within the aware and unaware categories, we group women according to education and occupation (e.g., employed or housewives) and include men for purposes of comparison (see Table 2.3). Among the less educated group, George McGovern did not fare well, irrespective of whether or not the woman was aware or not, or employed or not. As expected, there was a high precentage of nonvoting in this category, although most so for the unaware housewives, of whom 44 percent abstained. Although both men and women with only a high school education preferred Nixon to McGovern, this preference was especially pronounced among housewives whom we classified as aware. Here the preference cannot be explained by lack of information; they knew what McGovern stood for, and they did not like it. McGovern did even worse among unaware housewives, but since so many did not vote, little else can be said. It suffices to say that in this educational group, Nixon was the clear preference of men and women, and no extraordinary differences appear.

The interaction between gender, occupation, level of information, and education became more pronounced as we moved up the educational ladder. Here, McGovern gained substantial support among both housewives and aware employed women. Their support was in stark contrast to men, who gave McGovern less than a third of their vote. This male-female difference evaporates, however, when we consider the unaware respondents; they all preferred Nixon. Thus, awareness appears as a key variable; one that clearly separates men from women. Aware women with at least some college education, irrespective of employment, preferred McGovern. Men preferred Nixon.

In summary, McGovern's performance among women was not an affirmation of liberal commitment. His greatest support was among employed women with some post-high school education. Much of this support is found in the aware group. Yet there is some heterogeneity of response among women in comparison to men. Men, irrespective of education, preferred Nixon. Some women did prefer McGovern, but not enough to tip the scales. The extraordinary dissatisfaction with McGovern among college-educated housewives is of special interest. If support for McGovern is a rough barometer of feminist sympathies, the housewives were a major

TABLE 2.3
The 1972 Presidential Election: Gender, Education, and Awareness

	Panel-aware				Panel-unaware			
	Men	Women	Employed women	Housewives	Men	Women	Employed women	Housewives
ALL								
McGovern	27.6*	44.1	52.6	29.5	21.5	23.2	29.5	16.8
Nixon	57.7	40.4	36.8	52.3	55.4	47.9	47.7	49.7
Not voting	13.5	15.4	10.5	18.2	22.8	28.1	21.8	32.5
n	163	136	76	44	395	587	220	292
HIGH SCHOOL								
McGovern	30.4	30.6	35.3	22.7	21.9	20.8	26.0	15.1
Nixon	52.2	42.9	41.2	54.5	53.1	40.9	44.7	40.5
Not voting	17.4	26.5	23.5	22.7	25.0	38.0	28.5	44.4
n	46	49	17	22	224	379	123	205
SOME COLLEGE								
McGovern	18.5	56.3	57.6	54.5	20.5	28.7	35.3	23.0
Nixon	64.8	35.4	36.4	36.4	55.7	58.7	51.5	67.2
Not voting	14.8	8.3	6.1	9.1	23.0	10.5	13.2	4.9
n	54	48	33	11	122	143	68	61
COLLEGE								
McGovern	33.3	46.2	57.7	18.2	22.4	25.0	31.0	16.0
Nixon	55.6	43.6	34.6	63.6	65.3	64.1	51.7	80.0
Not voting	9.5	10.3	7.7	18.2	12.2	9.4	13.8	4.0
n	63	39	26	11	49	64	29	25

All entries are percentages. Columns may not sum to 100 percent because of rounding error or minor party candidates.

pocket of resistance in 1972. Clearly, there was no "woman's vote." Ironically, there was a "man's vote" in 1972. In no category did McGovern outpoll Nixon, nor were there substantial differences among the various categories of men.

The relatively poor showing of McGovern among women should be placed within an historical context. His nomination was due largely to the increasing significance of presidential primaries, and he was trailing Nixon in surveys from the nominating conventions to the election. The fact that some women nevertheless supported him is probably of equal significance to the fact that others did not.

In 1976, Jimmy Carter vowed to avoid McGovern's mistakes. He would not appeal to a narrow, ideologically committed segment of the population. He would campaign enigmatically, with fuzzy discussions of issues and maximum emphasis upon image—he was the "clean" outsider untainted by Watergate, who would bring morality back to government. He accomplished this feat remarkably well. Conservatives thought he was conservative and liberals thought he was liberal. A sympathetic media ignored his unimpressive record as governor of Georgia and boosted him early on in the campaign. About all he agreed to do if elected was not to lie—a welcome alternative to Nixon to be sure, but hardly the sort of campaign which encourages voters to make an issue-oriented choice. McGovern gambled on the alleged liberalism of women, youth, and others whose spokespersons conveyed the mistaken impression that the entire group was liberal, and he lost. Carter really had no ideology; he was a creature of the media and the presidential primary system.

Even with all this obfuscation, Carter did well among women. Employed women in the aware group, irrespective of education, gave him a majority (see Table 2.4). Aware housewives were more divided. In the aware group, housewives with a high school education and those with a college education opted for Ford; only those in the middle-education category preferred Carter. Unaware employed women with more than a high school education divided their vote about evenly. Similarly, educated unaware housewives showed a strong preference for Ford. Again, therefore, we cannot find a "women's vote." Men offer less of a puzzle. The less educated ones usually voted for Carter and the more educated ones normally voted for Ford (as one might expect, given the popular images of the parties). In the unaware group, education and Republican preference were also clearly related. Thus, men voted "normally," but women did not. For women, having a job is a good predictor of vote; for men, education is a good predictor. Thus Carter held his own among college-educated employed women, but suffered massive rejection by similarly educated housewives. Nevertheless in these three elections at least one generalization holds: *Employed women*

TABLE 2.4
The 1976 Presidential Election: Gender, Education, and Awareness

	Panel-aware				Panel-unaware			
	Men	Women	Employed women	Housewives	Men	Women	Employed women	Housewives
				ALL				
Ford	49.7*	39.3	32.9	50.0	37.9	36.0	37.2	37.4
Carter	38.3	46.7	56.6	38.1	38.5	36.7	43.2	31.5
Not voting	10.8	12.6	9.2	11.9	21.9	27.0	19.6	30.4
n	167	135	76	42	356	534	199	270
				HIGH SCHOOL				
Ford	26.1	36.2	23.5	50.0	29.6	26.7	31.5	26.3
Carter	56.5	40.4	58.8	35.0	43.2	38.4	42.6	35.1
Not voting	17.4	21.3	17.6	15.0	26.6	34.6	25.9	38.1
n	46	47	17	20	199	344	108	194
				SOME COLLEGE				
Ford	59.6	38.0	35.3	36.4	41.2	52.2	44.8	61.1
Carter	29.8	56.0	58.8	63.6	37.7	33.6	43.3	22.2
Not voting	10.5	6.0	5.9	.0	18.4	13.4	11.9	14.8
n	57	50	34	11	114	134	67	54
				COLLEGE				
Ford	57.8	44.7	36.0	63.6	67.4	53.6	41.7	77.3
Carter	32.8	42.1	52.0	18.2	18.6	33.9	45.8	22.7
Not voting	6.3	10.5	8.0	18.2	9.3	12.5	12.5	.0
n	64	38	25	11	43	56	24	22

*All entries are percentages. Columns may not sum to 100 percent because of rounding error or minor party candidates.

generally prefer Democratic candidates, while housewives do not. There are confounding effects (education and awareness in 1972 and 1976), but the generalization is still true. These variables are much more impressive in influencing women's votes than they are in influencing men's votes.

The story of 1980 can be told many different ways. Let us start with defections. It is now commonplace to observe that one major reason for Carter's defeat was the rejection of him personally. Although comparisons with 1976 are, strictly speaking, unfair, since Reagan did not run in that year, it is nevertheless true that Reagan captured most of the 1976 Ford vote while Carter did not do well in holding his 1976 vote. As Table 2.5 indicates, overall 81 percent of the 1976 Republican vote went to Reagan, but only 65 percent of the 1976 Democratic vote went to Carter. Carter lost least among employed women, but the differences between employed women, men, and housewives were not large. Men defected from Carter to Reagan at a higher level than women, but women defected from Carter to Anderson at a higher level than men. Women as well as men felt they were not better off in 1980 than they were in 1976. Women's responses to John Anderson are curious. He was the closet thing to the "liberal alternative" on the ballot. Yet employed women who voted for Anderson were drawn about equally from 1976 Republicans and 1976 Democrats. Among housewives, Anderson did gain more support among 1976 Carter voters. Possibly because he was not a genuine alternative, employed women did not provide his expected support, but overall he damaged the Democratic and Republican candidates in 1980 about equally, which is to say not very much.

But women did not punish Ronald Reagan. Feminist organizations were not pleased with Carter either, but certainly he was well known as the lesser of two evils. In this case, there was no substantial difference between housewives and employed women; both split their vote. Although women were not as enthusiastic about Reagan as men, their voting preferences roughly parallel men's preferences. Reagan did quite well in the traditional Republican coalition: Republican vote is clearly and strongly related to education (see Table 2.6). The more education, the higher the percentage of voters, irrespective of gender. Among those who had some college education, there is a discernible difference between men and women's voting choices, but not much difference between

TABLE 2.5
1976 Presidential Vote by 1980 Presidential Vote

		Reagan	Carter	Anderson	N
		\multicolumn{3}{c}{1980: ALL RESPONDENTS}	
1976	Ford	81.3*	11.1	7.6	368
	Carter	27.0	64.9	8.1	393
		\multicolumn{3}{c}{1980: MEN}	
1976	Ford	82.5	9.0	8.4	166
	Carter	32.4	61.9	5.8	173
		\multicolumn{3}{c}{1980: WOMEN}	
1976	Ford	80.2	12.9	6.9	202
	Carter	22.7	67.3	10.0	220
		\multicolumn{3}{c}{1980: EMPLOYED WOMEN}	
1976	Ford	79.4	9.8	10.8	102
	Carter	22.3	67.0	10.7	112
		\multicolumn{3}{c}{1980: HOUSEWIVES}	
1976	Ford	80.3	16.4	3.3	61
	Carter	25.9	63.8	10.3	58

*All entries are percentages.

housewives and employed women. In the best-educated group (where Reagan enjoyed his greatest support), women have caught up with men and the difference is trivial. Not too much can be said about the overwhelming Reagan support among college-educated housewives, due to the small number of respondents. The major point is that *Reagan's support increased with education.* College-educated employed women gave Reagan 47 percent of the vote, compared to 40 percent for employed women with some college, and only 30 percent of the high-school educated employed women. Anderson did best in the highest educated female group, but not any better (indeed slightly less) than was true of men.

In the least educated group, there is really no difference between men, employed women, and housewives. Reagan made his poorest showing here, where Democratic voting has been traditionally strongest. However, because nonvoting is also at its highest in the least educated group, Carter did not gain the advantage. We cannot say how the nonvoters would have voted; it is clear, however, that their nonparticipation denied Carter an advantage.

In 1980, as in the three previous elections, women did not vote cohesively; however, unlike the previous elections, education was a better predictor of vote in 1980 than was gender.

As we noted earlier, there does not appear to be any clear trend in the difference between the overall voting behavior of men and

TABLE 2.6
The 1980 Presidential Election: Gender and Education

	Total men	Total women	Employed women	Housewives
		HIGH SCHOOL		
Reagan	33.1*	28.8	30.7	31.1
Carter	28.3	29.6	28.4	26.7
Anderson	2.4	4.4	5.1	5.6
Not voting	36.1	37.3	35.8	36.6
n	332	504	215	161
		SOME COLLEGE		
Reagan	47.0	36.6	40.2	36.1
Carter	23.1	28.1	27.6	30.6
Anderson	8.2	7.2	9.2	2.8
Not voting	21.6	28.1	23.0	30.6
n	134	153	87	36
		COLLEGE		
Reagan	51.6	49.5	47.3	-†
Carter	23.0	32.1	35.1	-
Anderson	13.5	11.0	10.8	-
Not voting	11.9	7.3	6.8	-
n	126	109	74	-

†n too small for analysis.
*All entries are percentages. Columns may not sum to 100 percent of rounding error or minor party candidates.

women for president; the difference between the sexes in 1980 is about the same as it was in 1972. However, there is no denying the evidence that the 1980 election was significantly different from those dating back to Eisenhower's election in 1952. Regardless of whether or not there are differences between women and men in presidential voting behavior, these differences decline *the year after* the first election of a president, as shown by Gallup poll approval ratings. This was true of Eisenhower in 1953, Kennedy in 1961, Johnson in 1964, Nixon in 1969, Ford in 1975, and Carter in 1977. It was *not* true of Reagan in 1981.[7] The gap grew. In fact, by late 1983 a *New York Times*/CBS poll showed the gap to be 15 percentage points.

The judgment about whether or not Reagan's election in 1980 was the beginning of a trend in presidential election voting differences between men and women will have to await Reagan's passing from the American political landscape. There is, however, one trend that is evident—employed women and housewives are voting more alike. In 1972, the gap between housewives and employed women was about 13 percent. In 1976, the gap closed to about 7 percent, and in 1980 the gap all but disappeared. This, coupled with the fact that fewer and fewer women are identifying themselves as housewives, would seem to imply that women are becoming more homogeneous. Yet, as the analysis of Chapter 1 shows, this is not necessarily the case. Employed women and housewives are becoming more alike in their attitudes toward equality but substantial gaps remain. The diffusion of feminist ideology appears to have had its greatest impact upon the "housewife" image: The number of women willing to call themselves housewives has declined sharply. It has had a lesser impact upon narrowing the differences on equality issues between employed women and women still willing to identify themselves as housewives.

As we noted above, the 1980 election was different from previous presidential elections for which we have detailed polling data. Women and men have always consistently differed on the use of force. In the aftermath of World War II, women were less favorable than men to the United States joining NATO, more opposed to a continuance of the draft, and more opposed to using the atomic bomb. Women were less supportive of the Korean and Vietnam wars and opposed handguns and the death penalty more so than men did. On other issues—including those directly affecting women, such as abortion and the ERA—the differences between gender were not significant. "By the late 1970s, however, a big change was evident in the social and political responses of women and men. They had begun to take on the coloration of other groups in our society whose attitudes on a broad spectrum of issues are different. Differences of social and political outlook between men and women, while not huge, began appearing in a consistent pattern by the mid to late 1970s."[8] In addition to the traditional differences over the use of force, opinion pools began to show differences between the genders over government, aid to minority groups and the unemployed, over cleaning up the environment, and about confidence in the political system in general. Again, the differences were not huge, but they were new and appeared persistent.

Because these polls point to the 1980 election as a possible turning point, we will examine the issues of the presidential election of 1980 in detail during the next five sections of this chapter. We will then examine those issues that were also asked of respondents in the 1982 election study in order to plumb the outlines and the depth of the gender gap.

ISSUE SALIENCY IN 1980

One explanation for the similarity of voting between housewives and employed women is that there were other issues of greater importance than the equality issues which divided them. Even if Reagan was antifeminist, perhaps economic issues were of sufficient importance that his stance on women's issues was less important to women voters. The opportunity to investigate this possibility is enhanced by a question in the 1980 election study that was not asked in 1968, 1972, or 1976. In addition to indicating their preferences and beliefs, respondents were asked to indicate (on a scale of 0 to 100) how important an issue was to them. Thus, one may be in favor of the Equal Rights Amendment but consider it of less importance than, say, inflation. Under these circumstances, disagreement with a candidate's position on the Equal Rights Amendment would not be sufficient to cause one not to vote for him.

As indicated by Table 2.7, equal rights for women ranked dead last for the electorate as a whole. Far more important were the issues of defense spending, government spending in general, relations with the Soviet Union, and tax reductions. Curiously, inflation was of

TABLE 2.7
Issue Saliency in the 1980 Presidential Election

	All	Total men	Total women	Employed women	Housewives
Defense spending	82.16	82.74	81.59	82.25	81.06
Govt. spending	80.86	81.64	80.17	79.73	82.53
Inflation	76.77	76.08	77.50	76.56	77.40
Abortion	77.06	71.75	81.41	80.51	83.76
Tax cut	79.13	77.56	81.02	80.95	81.96
Govt. help minorities	75.69	75.51	75.86	74.42	78.59
Relations with U.S.S.R.	79.53	79.61	79.45	78.88	81.82
Eq. role women	73.91	69.72	77.48	80.63	74.38
Govt. guar. std. living	78.10	78.75	77.50	76.67	77.64

lesser importance. The poor showing of equal rights for women is matched by the low interest in helping minority groups. In 1980, the electorate had put aside the debates of the 1960s and 1970s. Questions of equity were no longer of major importance. The campaign was largely one of image, and when issues *were* discussed, they were largely problems of foreign policy and domestic spending. Nobody (except those directly affected) wanted to hear about inequality.

Men and women viewed the issues rather similarly: Both, for example, viewed defense spending as the most important issue in the election. However, although differences between the sexes were generally minor, on two feminist issues, abortion and an equal role for women, the differences were substantial (10 and 9 points, respectively). Further, the differences betweeen women were evident here. For housewives, abortion is the most important issue, while an equal role for women is the least important issue. For employed women, none of the women's issues is in first place; defense spending wins. However, employed women rated an equal role and abortion (along with tax cuts) just marginally behind defense spending. One interpretation of these findings is that employed women were more dispersed in their attitudes. Women's issues were important, but so were other issues which were of relevance to them as citizens. Employed women have priorities more like those of men. Perhaps they think less as women than as voters, a process of integration predicted by those who argue that, once women participate at a relatively equal rate with men, they will come to view issues and candidates with the same diversity as men do. Thus Anderson believes that "women are probably too cross-pressured ever to constitute a lasting political movement."[9] While the employed women's priorities do not fully support this thesis (they ranked women's issues higher than men did), 1980 did supply partial support for this idea.

Consider the differences in priorities between men and women and between housewives and employed women. The "within group" differences are greater than the "between group" differences on the issues of government spending, government help for minorities, and relations with the Soviet Union. None of these issues have a differential impact upon women. Since there is a greater variation within women as compared to men, there is no "women's position." Of the issues in which the differences are in the other direction, that is, when the differences between men and women exceed those between the groups of women, abortion and an equal role for women are the more conspicuous. However, there is also a substantial difference on inflation and a tax cut, two issues not directly linked to gender. The priorities of employed women, considered in the aggregate, are actually slightly more akin to those of men than they are to those of housewives.

To return to the fact that housewives place greatest importance on abortion and least importance on equal rights, while employed women place both relatively high, the standard deviations reveal a degree of consensus. Overall, standard deviations are highest for abortion and an equal role because of the substantial differences between women and men. However, employed women have the lowest standard deviation of the three groups on the equal role issue, and housewives have the lowest standard deviation on abortion. In other words, *employed women are unified about the importance of the equal role issues and housewives are unified on the importance of abortion.*

ISSUE SALIENCY AND THE VOTE IN 1980

Knowing that an issue is important to a group does not tell us anything about the actual voting preferences of that group. Abortion is important to both pro- and antiabortion organizations; and the fact that housewives rank it so highly does not mean that they are for abortion, nor does the high rank tell us whether they connected their preferences with those of the candidates. The next step is to find out how well an issue can predict a vote for Reagan or Carter. This is still the question of salience, with a new dimension. In Table 2.8, the entries are the difference between Carter and Reagan voters on a given issue. In addition to those included previously, other issues (about which questions of importance were not asked) are included. The higher the number, the greater the difference between Reagan and Carter voters; hence the greater the importance of an issue to the actual voting choice (as opposed to abstract importance). The largest difference was 100.[10]

No issue came close to government spending. The issue of big government, in the minds of the voters, was what the election was all

TABLE 2.8
Impact of the Issues upon Reagan versus Carter Voters

	Defense spending	Govt. spending	Inflation	Relax environ. regs.	Abortion Pre Election	Abortion Post Election	Tax cut	Govt. help minorities	U.S.S.R.	Eq. role women	Govt. std. living
All	22.0*	39.3	24.8	20.1	8.4	6.8	22.8	28.3	17.0	11.0	34.8
Total men	16.4	45.3	34.8	25.2	10.0	11.4	22.5	28.3	16.3	12.5	37.0
Total women	17.8	35.8	19.0	14.9	9.0	8.1	24.6	27.6	20.6	4.6	32.1
Employed women	27.8	33.0	17.5	10.0	13.2	13.0	20.3	23.8	19.0	17.3	25.5
Housewives	19.0	51.3	25.3	25.7	11.0	6.2	35.3	31.5	29.5	21.8	44.0

	ERA	Society discrim. ag. women	Build more N-plants	Control oil prices	School prayer	Busing	MEAN
All	32.2	11.4	14.5	23.9	5.4	22.8	19.1
Total men	30.4	10.2	22.1	29.3	0.2	23.5	21.0
Total women	33.2	16.9	4.6	18.2	10.9	23.4	18.0
Employed women	32.5	18.6	5.8	13.0	18.2	30.0	19.0
Housewives	38.6	13.0	4.2	24.3	9.2	19.8	22.7

*The higher the number, the greater the difference between Reagan and Carter voters on the issues. (Maximum possible value is 100.)

about. Reagan promised to "get the federal government off our backs," and hit a sensitive nerve. The spread between Carter and Reagan voters was 39; it was highest among housewives and men, and lowest among employed women. Irrespective of these differences, the issue was the clearest separator of Carter and Reagan supporters for all groups. With big government as the symbolic issue, it is hardly surprising that the next most discriminating issue also related to the role of the federal government: government guarantees of a good standard of living. All groups of voters agree on this ranking. Reagan's campaign theme resonated well, and he was not seriously impeded by antifeminist pronouncements. With the exception of the Equal Rights Amendment, issues of greatest concern to feminist organizations did not greatly affect women voters' choices.

It is somewhat surprising that other economic issues heavily emphasized by Reagan, such as inflation, tax cuts, and defense spending, did not make as much of an impact as the big government issues did. Reagan argued that big government causes inflation; that we have to increase defense spending in order to stand up to the Russians; and that tax cuts were the heart of "supply-side" economics, which promised new prosperity without inflation. These messages came through, but not so clearly as did the big government issues. Reagan's other issues did not do much better than busing, relaxing environmental regulations, and controlling the price of oil, problems which did not receive much campaign attention.

Finally, the least discriminating issues—abortion, school prayer, equal role for women, discrimination against women, and nuclear power—were rated trivial in comparison. Most of these were New Right or feminist issues. While the media may have give the impression of potent Moral Majority types and active feminist organizations mobilizing the political right and left, respectively, their issues just did not make much difference. An especially good example is nuclear power, a headline-grabbing issue (especially after Three-Mile Island), which Jerry Brown thought he could ride into the nomination. Although nuclear power attracts fiercely contending minorities, the issue was irrelevant to the mass of voters.

Table 2.8 is also useful as an indicator of group cohesion. Larger numbers indicate more cohesion within group polarization (i.e., polarization of the *voters* within the group). That is, on the issue of government spending (which generated the highest overall polarization), housewives are the most polarized group. They are also conspicuously polarized on whether or not the government should guarantee a decent standard living, the issue which produced the second highest overall polarization. In general, housewives are the most polarized group, and employed women are the least polarized group. The overall differences between the sexes (the mean column in Table 2.8), however, are not large.

ATTITUDES ON THE ISSUES AND THE VOTE IN 1980

We will select from the issues several representative ones. Our first analysis will include those issues which generated the greatest polarization: government spending and the role of the federal government in guaranteeing a decent standard of living. Then we will examine the issues of unusual importance to women, and conclude with a brief discussion of some of the nonpolarizing issues.

The most polarizing issue, government spending, should lay to rest any lingering notions that Reagan had a mandate to reduce government spending. Throughout his first few months in office, Reagan made frequent reference to several presumed mandates. Reagan was elected; he favored reduction of spending; ergo, there was a mandate to reduce spending. No mandate existed. David Stockman to the contrary, the electorate actually preferred *not* to reduce spending. Forty-three percent located themselves at points 5, 6, and 7 (don't reduce) while only 38 percent located themselves at points 1, 2, and 3 (reduce). Carter's problem was that Reagan got more of the vote among the budget cutters than Carter did among the status quo voters. Overall, support for Reagan was about 75 percent among those who placed themselves at the first three positions. However, support for Carter dropped from 70 percent at the extreme "don't cut" position to 53 percent at the more moderate positions. Those people who wanted to cut the budget, albeit a minority, *really wanted to do it and believed Reagan was the man for the job.* Those who wanted to keep spending at current levels were much less supportive of Carter. Government spending was viewed by the electorate as important; it was a polarizing issue, but the mandate was not there for Reagan.

The responses of women to the government spending question follow these rough contours (see Table 2.9). Recall that the issue was one which produced greater polarization among housewives than among employed women. Budget-cutting housewives were more enthusiastic about Reagan than were budget-cutting employed women; and, conversely, Carter did better among housewives who did not want to cut spending than he did among employed women with the same opinion. Table 2.9 clearly shows that Reagan's coalition among employed women was less firm. At the three scale positions favoring reduced spending, Reagan's percentage of the vote is lower among employed women than among housewives. Carter's major success among women was with those housewives who placed themselves at the extreme liberal end of the scale on spending. Their overwhelming preference for Carter contributes substantially to the polarization among housewives.

In the aggregate, employed women were the least likely to prefer a reduction of federal spending (32 percent locate at the first three points); men the most likely (44 percent); with housewives between the two extremes (37 percent). Employed women were the most liberal group of voters; and those of them who were not liberal did not support Reagan to the same degree as did other groups. Still, Carter was not an attractive enough alternative.

Lest we assume that employed women are uniformly more liberal, another polarizing question, whether or not the government should guarantee jobs and a good standard of living, lays this

TABLE 2.9
Government Spending

		Employed women				Housewives			
		Reagan	Carter	Anderson	n	Reagan	Carter	Anderson	n
Reduce†	1	66.7*	26.7	6.7	15	77.8	11.1	11.1	9
	2,3	77.0	14.8	8.2	61	83.9	12.9	3.2	31
	4	50.0	40.4	9.6	52	30.4	56.5	13.0	23
	5,6	37.5	48.8	13.8	80	37.0	48.1	14.8	27
Don't Reduce	7	27.3	66.7	6.1	33	17.7	82.4	0.0	17

*All entries are percentages. Rows may not sum to 100 because of rounding.
†1 = Government should provide many fewer services; reduce spending a lot.
7 = Government should continue to provide services; no reduction in spending.

assumption to rest. A plurality of housewives favored both a reduction of government spending and the federal government guaranteeing a decent standard of living for everyone. However, the work ethic is more prominent among employed women (and men). It is interesting that women who are employed and vote are more likely to accept some form of social Darwinism. They are not the rugged individualists men claim to be, but they certainly are more willing to let each person get along on his or her own than are housewives. Almost 47 percent of employed women, as opposed to 46 percent of men and 42 percent of housewives, placed themselves at scale positions 5, 6, and 7 (government let each person get ahead on own). Even those employed women who strongly believed that the government should guarantee a good standard of living did not accept Carter to the same degree as did housewives (see Table 2.10).

The question is not really fair, since neither candidate promised such massive intervention; however, Reagan's rhetoric certainly lent itself to a laissez-faire interpretation. Reagan did not propose that each person should be left along to sink or swim, nor did Carter propose complete social and economic equality. Differences between presidential candidates are rarely that severe.

Carter's relatively poor showing among those in ideological sympathy with him appears here also. Reagan gets strong support from those at positions 5, 6, and 7; Carter gets substantially less

TABLE 2.10
Government Jobs and Standard of Living

		Employed women				Housewives			
		Reagan	Carter	Anderson	n	Reagan	Carter	Anderson	n
Job†	1	26.7*	66.7	6.7	15	5.6	94.4	0.0	18
	2,3	32.7	51.9	15.4	52	33.3	50.0	16.7	24
	4	41.4	43.1	15.5	58	56.0	40.0	4.0	25
	5,6	58.8	34.1	7.1	85	73.7	18.4	7.9	38
On own	7	80.0	20.0	0.0	25	72.7	27.3	0.0	11

*All entries are percentages. Rows may not sum to 100 because of rounding.
†1 = Government see to a job and good standard of living.
7 = Government let each person get ahead on own.

support among voters at positions 1, 2, and 3. However, among housewives, this is not the case: Carter does just about as well among his adherents as does Reagan. Here again, ideology is a better predictor of the vote of housewives than it is for employed women.

It is curious that inflation was not an especially salient issue, nor especially polarizing (see Table 2.11). Given subsequent events, and Reagan's unshaken belief that a reduction of government spending and revenues would defeat inflation, one might have supposed that the 1980 electorate would be unusually responsive. Such was not the case. Perhaps no one had any strong beliefs in 1980 about whether or not a particular course of action, or indeed any action, could substantially reduce inflation. More general surveys indicated that belief that Reagan's programs would reduce inflation was high during the first month or so of his term in office, but abated as inflation continued to ravage the economy. Unlike other issues related to federal spending and performance, the electorate is clustered away from the extremes on the inflation issue. The 1980 electorate really did not know whether it was more important to reduce inflation or to reduce unemployment.

The unemployment issue typically helps Democratic candidates. The fact that the electorate viewed unemployment as no more serious than inflation did Carter no good. In fact, he was doubly

TABLE 2.11
Inflation

		Employed women				Housewives			
		Reagan	Carter	Anderson	n	Reagan	Carter	Anderson	n
Reduce†	1	85.7*	14.3	0.0	7	-	-	-	-[a]
Inflation	2,3	57.1	33.3	9.5	42	75.0	18.8	6.3	16
	4	53.2	41.9	4.8	62	48.5	39.4	12.1	33
Reduce	5,6	42.1	45.6	12.3	57	50.0	37.5	12.5	8
Unemploy.	7	16.7	83.3	0.0	12	0.0	100.0	0.0	5

*All entries are percentages. Rows may not sum to 100 because of rounding.
†1 = Reduce inflation even if unemployment goes up a lot.
 7 = Reduce unemployment even if inflation goes up a lot.
[a] n too small for analysis.

hurt, because even those voters who thought unemployment more serious than inflation gave Reagan a hefty proportion of the vote. If we exclude the extremes, the greatest proportions of the nonneutral located at points 2 and 3 and at points 5 and 6. Reagan did better than Carter in mobilizing his natural constituency. Reagan took 41 percent of the voters who thought unemployment more serious than inflation, while Carter took only 20 percent of the voters more worried about inflation than unemployment.

There were some rather pronounced differences in the willingness of the various groups of voters to transfer their attitude on inflation into a vote. For example, one would expect that, if an issue was important in a voting choice, the people who vote for a candidate would disproportionately support the position on (or direction of) an issue which is most closely associated with the ideology of the candidate. Inflation did not have such a strong effect. Carter did best in his natural constituency (reduce unemployment) among his men voters, next best among employed women, and poorest among housewives. Reagan was weakest in his natural constituency (reduce inflation) among employed women.

A contrasting pattern of preference appeared on the matter of tax reduction. Reagan was officially committed to the Kemp-Roth tax reduction plan, which required a 30 percent reduction in federal taxes over three years. The electorate was not asked to judge some of the more subtle variations (such as whether the reduction should be across the board). They were asked simply to indicate the magnitude of the reduction preferred. No option to increase taxes (perhaps on the rich) was offered, so the question was modestly loaded. Here again, the mood of the electorate and the rhetoric of the Republican candidate were well synchronized. Supply-siders (that is, those favoring cuts of at least 30 percent) outnumbered the "no cut" voters. For the electorate as a whole, 35 percent were supply-siders and one-fourth were "no cut" voters. The greatest support for supply-side economics was found among housewives and employed women, with men more equally divided. Reagan's support among supply-siders ran in the same direction: He received support from 38 percent of the male supply-siders, 45 percent from the employed women supply-siders, and 53 percent from the housewives who favored massive tax cuts (see Table 2.12). The greater the proclivity for supply-side economics, the greater the support for Reagan.

TABLE 2.12
Federal Tax Reduction

	Employed women				Housewives			
	Reagan	Carter	Anderson	n	Reagan	Carter	Anderson	n
No cut	42.9*	50.0	7.1	42	13.3	66.7	20.0	15
10%	35.5	48.4	16.1	31	35.7	42.9	21.4	14
20%	51.1	33.3	15.6	45	69.2	30.8	0.0	13
30%	68.9	24.4	6.7	45	65.2	30.4	4.4	23
Over 30%	52.2	39.1	8.7	23	42.9	57.1	0.0	7

*All entries are percentages. Rows may not sum to 100 because of rounding.

This issue helps to explain why Reagan did relatively well among women. Women's economic philosophy is mixed. There is a modest tendency for women to prefer some of the philosophical positions of the Democrats. They are less likely to want a reduction in government expenditures and they are less likely to be advocates of rugged individualism. However, employed women are not necessarily more liberal than housewives: They are less interested in reducing government expenditures, but are slightly more likely to believe that every person should be left on his or her own. On the other economic issues, inflation and tax reduction, women are either indistinguishable from men (inflation) or are more likely to prefer the Republican program (tax cuts). The latter issue is especially pronounced in this regard.

One aspect of the 1980 election contradicts widely held opinions about women. It has long been believed that women are more pacific than men. As we noted above, they were more dovish about the Vietnam and Korea conflicts, for example. As Baxter and Lansing conclude, "A pattern stands clear over twenty-five years: women have been more opposed to the use of force and to the support of warlike policies."[11] Explanations range from biological destiny (women bear life and are more reluctant to support policies which risk it) to socialization (women are encouraged to be more pacific by social institutions such as schools). Whatever the explanation, women's attitudes are thought to be durable. In 1980, however, the stability of such attitudes could be questioned. Women were just about as likely as men to think that trying to get along with the Russians was a "big mistake" (see Table 2.13). Some evidence of the socialization argument may be evident in the fact that housewives

TABLE 2.13
Should We Try Harder to Get Along with U.S.S.R.?

		OVERALL			
		Total men	Total women	Employed women	Housewives
Try^a	1	13.7*	12.5	11.2	15.2
	2,3	27.5	26.8	28.4	33.0
	4	21.4	25.7	28.0	24.1
	5,6	26.2	26.1	26.3	18.8
Mistake	7	11.2	8.9	6.0	8.9
	n	393	440	232	112

		BY CANDIDATES							
		Reagan	Carter	Anderson	n	Reagan	Carter	Anderson	n
		Total men				Total women			
Try	1	51.9†	44.4	3.7	54	21.8	69.1	9.1	55
	2,3	50.9	38.9	10.2	108	45.8	42.4	11.9	118
	4	56.0	36.9	7.1	84	54.9	37.2	8.0	113
	5,6	68.9	22.3	8.7	103	61.7	29.6	8.7	115
Mistake	7	59.1	27.3	13.6	44	64.1	30.8	5.1	39
		Employed women				Housewives			
Try	1	30.8	61.5	7.7	26	11.8	76.5	11.8	17
	2,3	45.5	42.4	12.1	66	16.2	81.1	2.7	37
	4	55.4	33.9	10.8	65	63.0	37.0	0.0	27
	5,6	63.9	26.2	9.8	61	66.7	23.8	9.5	21
Mistake	7	64.1	30.8	5.1	14	90.0	10.0	0.0	10

*All entries are percentages. Columns may not sum to 100 because of rounding.
†Rows may not sum to 100 because of rounding.
^{a}1 = Important to try very hard to get along with U.S.S.R.
7 = Big mistake to try harder to get along with U.S.S.R.

are somewhat more likely than employed women to want to try to get along with the Russians. However, the difference, though significant, is hardly compelling. Of course, it was difficult not to get caught up in the frenzy of an election when one of the candidates

TABLE 2.14
Defense Spending

		OVERALL			
		Total men	Total women	Employed women	Housewives
Decrease[a]	1	2.2*	2.6	2.5	1.7
	2,3	7.2	9.0	11.1	8.7
	4	13.4	20.0	18.5	20.9
	5,6	53.7	47.4	46.1	46.1
Increase	7	23.5	20.9	21.8	22.6
	n	404	454	243	115

		BY CANDIDATES							
		Reagan	Carter	Anderson	n	Reagan	Carter	Anderson	n
		Total men				Total women			
Decrease	1	22.2†	55.6	22.2	9	8.3	83.3	8.3	12
	2,3	31.0	62.1	6.9	29	22.0	53.7	24.4	41
	4	50.0	42.6	7.4	54	39.6	46.2	14.3	91
	5,6	60.8	29.5	9.7	217	58.1	34.9	7.0	215
Increase	7	62.1	30.5	7.4	95	63.2	35.8	1.0	95
		Employed women				Housewives			
Decrease	1	16.7	83.3	0.0	6	-	-	-	-
	2,3	14.8	55.6	29.6	27	30.0	60.0	10.0	10
	4	37.8	46.7	15.6	45	50.0	37.5	12.5	24
	5,6	61.6	31.3	7.1	112	60.4	30.2	9.4	53
Increase	7	69.8	28.3	1.9	53	50.0	50.0	0.0	26

*All entries are percentages. Columns may not sum to 100 because of rounding.
†Rows may not sum to 100 because of rounding.
[a]1 = Greatly decrease defense spending. 7 = Greatly increase defense spending.

consistently described the Soviet Union as the source of all evil and pledged to arm us to the teeth to thwart them. It may be remarkable that a plurality of voters, male and female, still wanted us to "try harder." Perhaps the question does not tap the same reservoir of pacificism that previous questions did, coming as they did during actual military combat. Still, one would have thought that women would have been more inclined toward cooperation. The strongest evidence in support of the idea that women are more inclined toward less belligerent foreign policies is that women who were inclined toward cooperation with the Soviet Union were more supportive of Carter than men were. It is noteworthy that this tendency is most pronounced among housewives, who are more pacific than employed women.

Trying to get along with the Russians is one thing; arming to the teeth is quite another. Table 2.14 shows that large majorities of men *and* women wanted to increase defense spending; differences between the sexes were minor, as were differences between employed women and housewives. If we equate decreased defense expenditures with a pacific position, there is little evidence to support the idea that women are less belligerent. Voters translated their desires into candidate preference quite well: Support for Reagan increased as support for defense spending increased, and women supporting this were as enthusiastic about Reagan as men supporting it. Whether or not 1980 was an aberration remains to be seen. Perhaps Carter did not offer a competitive alternative to an aggressive foreign policy. Nevertheless, the 1980 election clearly established that women, whatever their patterns of socialization, *can* be as nationalistic as men. This did not persist in 1982 (see Tables 2.13 and 2.14).

Another belief which has achieved substantial support is that women are more humane, that they are more sympathetic to the plight of the disadvantaged. Baxter and Lansing conclude that ". . . women have been more supportive of efforts to achieve racial equality than have men."[12] Judging solely by the 1980 election, this conclusion is unwarranted. Again, the rhetoric may have influenced opinion. Neverthless, women were indistinguishable from men. Table 2.15 shows that no one was very enthusiastic about helping minorities. The phrase "women and minorities," used so often in discussing discrimination, may be inappropriate. Women do not identify with minorities, if their attitudes in 1980 are any indication.

TABLE 2.15
Government Help for Minorities

		OVERALL			
		Total men	Total women	Employed women	Housewives
Help†	1	4.6*	5.3	2.7	6.1
	2,3	16.5	15.7	17.6	12.2
	4	26.2	32.3	32.2	31.3
Not	5,6	38.8	33.6	34.1	36.5
Help	7	13.9	13.2	13.3	13.9
	n	389	470	255	115

*All entries are percentages. Columns may not sum to 100 because of rounding.
†1 = Government should help minority groups. 7 = Minority groups should help themselves.

Women not only opposed the abstract notion of "helping minorities," but they also came out foursquare against busing—a specific effort to alleviate the plight of minorities. One study reported that, in 1964, 25 percent of women approved of busing.[13] In 1980, only 10 percent of employed women and 8 percent of housewives supported busing (positions 1, 2, and 3); about 85 percent opposed it. Indeed, 57 percent of employed women and an astonishing 71 percent of housewives were opposed (compared to 58 percent of men). The only possible support for the idea that women are more humane in their attitude toward the disadvantaged is the very weak argument that Reagan fared comparatively poorly among housewives extremely opposed to busing. Since he still carried a majority of the extreme antibusing housewives, the argument is far from compelling.

Of all the "humane issues," the environment proved to be the only one to produce a clear male-female difference.[14] Women, especially housewives, opposed any relaxation of existing standards, while men were more inclined to relax them (see Table 2.16). The differences are not great, but a majority of women favored the status quo and a majority of men did not. Unfortunately for Carter, the environmentalists found Reagan just about as attractive. All voters, including women, who wanted to preserve the status quo divided equally; however, Reagan received strong support from antienvironmental voters.

The same phenomenon can be observed in voter response to nuclear power. The differences between women and men in Table 2.17 are huge, eclipsing all other issues. Fifty-three percent of male voters wanted to build more nuclear plants, compared with 25 percent of employed women and 30 percent of housewives. But antinuclear voters did not abandon Reagan to any appreciable degree. Among employed women, the strongest antinuclear bloc, Reagan actually did better than Carter among those who preferred the status quo. Reagan split the vote of the antinuclear employed women. Housewives, only slightly less opposed to nuclear plants,

TABLE 2.16
Should Environmental Regulations Be Relaxed?

		OVERALL			
		Total men	Total women	Employed women	Housewives
Unchanged†	1	45.7*	57.7	57.4	58.3
Relax W/Q	2	15.8	12.7	10.0	13.0
Relax	3	38.4	29.6	32.7	28.7
n		398	456	251	108

		BY CANDIDATES							
		Reagan	Carter	Anderson	n	Reagan	Carter	Anderson	n
		Total men				Total women			
Unchanged	1	44.0	45.1	11.0	182	43.7	44.7	11.8	263
Relax W/Q	2	69.8	23.8	6.3	63	67.2	27.6	5.2	58
Relax	3	68.6	25.5	5.9	153	59.3	37.0	3.7	135
		Employed women				Housewives			
Unchanged	1	44.4	41.7	13.9	144	44.4	46.0	9.5	63
Relax W/Q	2	64.0	32.0	4.0	25	78.6	21.4	0.0	14
Relax	3	58.5	39.0	2.4	82	67.7	25.8	6.5	31

*All entries are percentages. Columns and rows may not sum to 100 because of rounding.
†1 = Keep regulations unchanged. 2 = Relax regulations with qualifications. 3 = Relax regulations.

showed no relationship between their attitude and their vote. Pronuclear males gave Reagan his strongest support, but their support was only marginally higher than that of women.

Thus, although the environmental issue, especially nuclear power, produced distinctly different responses from each gender, it did not produce a women's vote. In this, as in the other issues not directly related to the status of women, Carter was an unpalatable alternative. John Anderson did steal some votes from Carter among women, but not among men. Anderson's relatively high support among antinuclear women does little to dispel his stereotype as the favorite of the "chablis and Brie" set; antinuclear employed women

TABLE 2.17
Should More Nuclear Power Plants Be Built?

		OVERALL			
		Total men	Total women	Employed women	Housewives
Build More[a]	1	53.0*	27.4	25.1	30.2
Status Quo	2	34.0	52.8	50.2	57.8
Shut Down	3	13.0	19.8	24.7	12.1
n		409	470	255	116

		BY CANDIDATES							
		Reagan	Carter	Anderson	n	Reagan	Carter	Anderson	n
		Total men				Total women			
Build More[a]	1	65.0	25.8	9.2	217	55.8	38.8	5.4	129
Status Quo	2	46.8	44.6	8.6	189	49.6	42.7	7.7	248
Shut Down	3	45.3	47.2	7.5	53	41.9	41.9	16.1	93
		Employed women				Housewives			
Build More	1	57.8	37.5	4.7	64	57.1	37.1	5.7	35
Status Quo	2	50.0	40.6	9.4	128	53.7	38.8	7.5	67
Shut Down	3	41.3	42.9	15.9	63	57.1	28.6	14.3	14

*All entries are percentages. Columns and rows may not sum to 100 because of rounding.
[a] 1 = Favor building more plants. 2 = Operating only those already built. 3 = See all plants closed down.

found him most attractive. Anderson did not make any appreciable difference on more broadly based economic and social issues. He did find somewhat of a home on the nuclear issue.

If women were dissatisfied with the option offered by Carter on these economic, foreign policy, social, and environmental issues, they should have had no trouble deciding on the "lesser of two evils" when the candidates discussed issues of concern to women. Whatever Carter may not have said or done, it was clear that Reagan had a more traditional attitude about the appropriate role of women. He opposed the Equal Rights Amendment, while maintaining that the same end could be achieved by different (unspecified) means. Both were fuzzy on abortion; Carter's nascent fundamentalism kept him from exploiting Reagan's unabashed opposition.

In spite of such waffling in the election, the electorate of 1980 was substantially more willing to accept the idea that men and women should have equal roles than was the case when the question was first asked in 1972. About half the voters in 1972 placed themselves at the egalitarian end of the scale (positions 1, 2,, and 3); in 1980, two-thirds of the voters did so. Reagan thus appeared to be a bit out of touch. However, the electorate did not accord Carter an advantage. In fact, Reagan outpolled him at every position on the equal-role scale except for position 7, those who believed that a women's place was in the home. Although it seems absurd, *the most traditional voters preferred Carter.* Perhaps his homey image and conspicuous concern with matters religious and familial stood him in good stead. This bizarre result is not quite so apparent with women voters: Carter did outpoll Reagan at the extreme egalitarian position. In fact, he won a majority of the egalitarian housewives' votes (see Table 2.18). Yet Reagan lost badly at the most traditional point among employed women and split with Carter at the same scale point among housewives.

Imposing additional controls does not help clarify the issue. Since we know that employed women are more egalitarian than housewives, and highly educated employed women more egalitarian than poorly educated employed women, we could hypothesize that education combines with occupational status to reveal expected relationships. That is not the case. Among college-educated employed women, Reagan outpolled Carter 44 percent to 40 percent when we control for position on the seven-point scale. The most egalitarian, that is, the college-educated employed women, still

TABLE 2.18
Equal Role for Women

		EMPLOYED WOMEN				HOUSEWIVES			
		Reagan	Carter	Anderson	n	Reagan	Carter	Anderson	n
Equal†	1	40.2*	44.9	15.0	107	39.4	51.5	9.1	33
Role	2,3	54.3	37.0	8.6	81	59.0	35.9	5.1	39
	4	63.4	34.2	2.4	41	40.9	45.5	13.6	22
Place	5,6	74.3	17.1	8.6	35	75.0	25.0	0.0	24
in Home	7	36.4	63.6	0.0	11	45.5	45.5	9.1	11

*All entries are percentages. Rows may not sum to 100 because of rounding.
†1 = Equal role. 7 = Women's place is in home.

preferred Reagan. High-school educated housewives, the most traditional group, went to Reagan by a two-thirds margin. However, high-school educated, traditional, employed women actually preferred Carter (48 to 40). All in all, female voters did not identify Reagan as the enemy of equality or, if they did, they did not vote on that basis.

Respondents were allowed to react to the statement, "Our society discriminates against women." Belief in discrimination is more characteristic of employed women than of men or of housewives. Forty-two percent of employed women strongly agreed, compared to less than one-third of men or housewives. Among the respondents who strongly agreed, Carter enjoyed the voting edge among employed women, but his advantage was not very great; it was even less among housewives. (See Table 2.19). Still, the fact that women who were highly conscious of discrimination bucked the tide and supported Carter is not to be sneered at—especially since men who strongly agreed that women are discriminated against preferred Reagan. Carter's problem was that the margin was slight even among those who agreed strongly; possibly the relatively strong showing of Anderson among voters who believed that discrimination against women was pervasive hurt Carter. However, even more damaging was the fact that, once you leave this single extreme category, Reagan did quite well. He edged out Carter among employed women who agreed less strongly and outscored him heavily among housewives with the same belief. There is a clear relationship between belief in the reality of discrimination and support for Carter. The problem is that Carter did not do as well as one might have expected. Reagan's worst showing, among employed women who strongly agree that society discriminated against women, is still rather healthy.

The symbolic corrective to discrimination is the Equal Rights Amendment, the focus of much debate since its approval by Congress almost a decade ago. There is a clear relationship between support for the Amendment and support for Carter. The majority of voters who supported the Amendment strongly, whether men, employed women, or housewives, voted for Carter. The majority of voters who opposed it voted for Reagan. However, Carter was afflicted by the same problem described above. Those who strongly opposed the Amendment were far more supportive of Reagan than strong supporters, in turn, supported Carter. Thus, there was a virtual tie among women who approved the Amendment with less enthusiasm, and a sweep for Reagan among strong disapprovers. For example, among the 31 percent of employed women who strongly approved the ERA, Carter received 57 percent; among the 23 percent who strongly disapproved, Reagan got 79 percent (see Table 2.20). Hence, the greater percentage of a smaller percentage meant that Reagan more than held his own. Carter was hurt by Anderson's strong showing among approvers while Reagan had no such problem among those who opposed with vehemence. There is

TABLE 2.19
Does Our Society Discriminate Against Women?

		EMPLOYED WOMEN				HOUSEWIVES			
		Reagan	Carter	Anderson	n	Reagan	Carter	Anderson	n
Agree†	1	38.4*	45.5	16.1	112	44.4	47.2	8.3	36
	2	47.6	44.4	7.9	63	55.2	34.5	10.3	29
	3	66.7	27.5	5.9	51	55.6	38.9	5.6	36
Disagree	4	62.5	35.0	2.5	40	62.1	31.0	6.9	29

*All entries are percentages. Rows may not sum to 100 because of rounding.
†1 = Strongly agree. 2 = Not strongly agree. 3 = Not strongly disagree. 4 = Strongly disagree.

no denying that Reagan mobilized his constituency. His greatest support was among housewives who strongly opposed the Amendment (87 percent of 21 percent), while Carter's source of greatest support was employed women who strongly approved (57 percent of 31 percent). Even if we assign Carter all the votes stolen by Anderson among employed women who strongly approved, he still does not equal Reagan's support among strongly opposed housewives.

Finally, the abortion issue did very little for Carter. There were two abortion questions included in the 1980 survey, one before and one after the election. Both reveal identical patterns. However, the sensitivity of the issue is well illustrated by shifts in opinion between the first and second interviews. The sample appears less committed to abortion in the second interview, probably because the questions are phrased differently. The second interview introduced the word "child" in the proabortion options. Therefore, the percentage of

TABLE 2.20
Support for the Equal Rights Amendment

		OVERALL	
		Employed women	Housewives
Approve[a]	1	31.1*	29.4
	2	29.9	26.6
	3	16.1	22.9
Disapprove	4	22.8	21.1
n		465	109

		BY CANDIDATES							
		Employed women				Housewives			
		Reagan	Carter	Anderson	n	Reagan	Carter	Anderson	n
Approve	1	26.6†	57.0	16.5	79	34.4	56.3	9.4	32
	2	44.7	43.4	11.8	76	41.4	44.8	13.8	29
	3	58.5	34.1	7.3	41	64.0	24.0	12.0	25
Disapprove	4	79.3	17.2	3.4	58	87.0	13.0	0.0	23

*All entries are percentages. Columns may not sum to 100 because of rounding.
†Rows may not sum to 100 because of rounding.
[a]1 = Strongly approve. 2 = Not strongly approve. 3 = Not strongly disapprove. 4 = Strongly disapprove.

people selecting the extreme proabortion position fell. This difference aside, the degree to which Reagan did well among proabortion voters is striking (see Tables 2.21 and 2.22). There is a virtual dead heat among both employed women and housewives at position 4 (proabortion), while Carter's fundamentalism appears to help him among antiabortionists. Notice that while Reagan carried the antiabortion vote among men and employed women, Carter won the day among antiabortion housewives. Since the same pattern occurs on both questions, it is obvious that more traditional voters (e.g., housewives) responded in a unique fashion. Men's attitude toward abortion is not relevant to their voting choice. Note also that while Anderson probably damaged Carter among proabortion voters, he did not do so among the antiabortion

TABLE 2.21
Abortion: Pre-Election Question

		Reagan	Carter	Anderson	n	Reagan	Carter	Anderson	n
		Total men				Total women			
Restrictive†	1	56.3*	41.7	2.1	48	45.5	52.7	1.8	55
	2	54.2	41.2	4.6	131	52.4	44.0	3.6	168
	3	65.9	26.1	8.0	88	58.3	35.7	6.0	84
Permissive	4	50.4	35.7	14.0	143	40.8	43.8	15.4	201
		Employed women				Housewives			
Restrictive	1	57.9	42.1	0.0	19	45.0	55.0	0.0	20
	2	50.6	45.7	3.7	81	60.8	35.3	3.9	51
	3	64.8	27.8	7.4	54	45.5	45.5	9.1	11
Permissive	4	41.0	42.7	16.2	117	43.5	41.3	15.2	46

*All entries are percentages. Rows may not sum to 100 because of rounding.
†1 = By law, abortion should never be permitted.
2 = The law should permit abortion only in the case of rape, incest, or when the woman's life is in danger.
3 = The law should permit abortion for reasons *other than* rape, incest, or danger to the woman's life, but only after the need for the abortion has been clearly established.
4 = By law, a woman should always be able to obtain an abortion as a matter of personal choice.

housewives. Obviously, they were responding to Carter's fundamentalist image.

There is one inescapable conclusion from all these various matchings of attitudes and votes. Carter could not offset Reagan's advantage on economic issues by attracting women who supported "their" issues. He did fairly well, but not well enough. Ironically, his fuzziness was a handicap. In 1976, liberals thought he was liberal and conservatives thought he was conservative. In 1980, with Reagan mounting a right-wing challenge, Carter could not offer a clear alternative.

1980 marked the first serious electoral activity by the Moral Majority and other fundamentalist groups. Reagan resonated well with such groups. However, Carter could not be counted out, given what we have seen about his appeal to the morally conservative. The

TABLE 2.22
Abortion: Post-Election Question

		Reagan	Carter	Anderson	n	Reagan	Carter	Anderson	n
			Total men				Total women		
Restrictive†	1	58.1*	35.5	6.5	31	49.0	49.0	2.0	51
	2	54.2	41.1	4.7	192	53.5	42.2	4.3	230
	3	66.3	22.9	10.8	83	54.2	38.9	6.9	72
Permissive	4	49.5	35.2	15.2	105	38.4	43.9	17.7	164
			Employed women				Housewives		
Restrictive†	1	60.0	40.0	0.0	25	43.8	56.2	0.0	16
	2	54.1	41.3	4.6	109	53.1	42.2	4.7	64
	3	59.5	28.6	11.9	42	60.0	40.0	0.0	15
Permissive	4	36.8	45.3	17.9	95	47.4	34.2	18.4	38

*All entries are percentages. Rows may not sum to 100 because of rounding.
†1 = Abortion should never be permitted.
2 = Abortion should be permitted only if the life and health of the woman is in danger.
3 = Abortion should be permitted if, due to personal reasons, the woman would have difficulty in caring for the child.
4 = Abortion should never be forbidden, since one should not require a woman to have a child she doesn't want.

fundamentalist groups were not without support. A hefty 46 percent of the electorate believed that the Bible was "God's work" and contained no errors. A majority of housewives were of this opinion, as were 47 percent of employed women. As might be expected, Anderson made his strongest showing among the unbelievers, few as they might have been. Among those voters who believed that the Bible is no more than a "good book," Anderson garnered 28 percent, his strongest showing, and Reagan's poorest. On the other hand, Carter's homespun Bible-thumping, God-fearing image salvaged something. Housewives, the majority of whom believe that the Bible is literally true, gave Carter 46 percent, his best showing in these categories. Nevertheless, fundamentalist sentiment was clearly in Reagan's direction.

Women are more sensitive to religious questions than are men. This sensitivity is well illustrated by the question of prayer in schools. In spite of Supreme Court decisions, an overwhelming majority—nearly 75 percent—wants to allow schools to start each day with a prayer. For men, the question was completely unrelated to electoral choice. Both proponents and opponenets of prayer supported Reagan (see Table 2.23). There were substantial differences among women. The opponents of prayer were unusually

TABLE 2.23
School Prayer

	Reagan	Carter	Anderson	n
		Total Men		
Prayer[†]	59.9*	38.2	5.9	238
No Prayer[a]	51.4	35.5	13.1	107
		Employed women		
Prayer	57.5	37.9	4.6	174
No Prayer	25.9	53.7	20.4	54
		Housewives		
Prayer	51.7	42.7	5.6	89
No Prayer	32.0	48.0	20.0	25

*All entries are percentages. Row may not sum to 100 because of rounding.
[†]Schools should be allowed to start each day with a prayer.
[a]Religion does not belong in schools.

hostile to Reagan, and unusually sympathetic to Carter and Anderson. This religious conservatism, and the willingness to relate it to voting choice, clearly distinguishes women from men.

1980: MANDATE FOR REAGAN OR REJECTION OF CARTER?

It seems that after every presidential election the winner interprets his victory as a mandate for the policies he advocated during the election. Lyndon Johnson interpreted his landslide victory over Barry Goldwater in 1964 as an endorsement of his plans for a Great Society. The source of the mandate for the dramatic escalation of the Vietnam war in 1965 is less clear. Before the Watergate avalanche began in the spring of 1973, Richard Nixon clearly interpreted his victory as a mandate to concentrate even more authority in the White House. (Remember all the talk in January and February 1973 about the Supercabinet, impoundment, constitutional crisis, and one-man rule.) In 1980, Ronald Reagan saw his victory as a mandate for supply-side economics—massive tax cuts and sharp reductions in government spending.

The public agreed with Reagan about the importance of these issues (Table 2.7) and concern over government spending clearly differentiated Reagan and Carter voters (Table 2.8). Yet, overall, 20 percent of the voting public was neutral on the main issue of the election, 43 percent did not want to reduce spending, and 38 percent did want to cut back. This does not mean the public was not in sync with Reagan's attitudes. Cutting government spending can mean cutting defense spending and Reagan campaigned hard on the theme of *increasing* defense spending (for which the public was overwhelmingly in favor). Perhaps more to the point is the issue of the government seeing to it that everyone has a job and a good standard of living. Ever since the New Deal, Democrats and Republicans have been at odds over the role of government in providing employment. In 1980, the voting public was clearly on Reagan's side of the issue. Half the public wanted people to get ahead on their own, 21 percent were neutral, and only 29 percent favored government action. The issue of whether or not the government should help minority groups (i.e., blacks and Hispanics) was closely related to the jobs issue, and it shows a very similar pattern of support. Overall, Reagan's antibig-government theme (except, of course, for defense) was clearly in tune with a majority of the voting public.

TABLE 2.24
Government Jobs and Standard of Living: 1972-1980

		Total men	Total women	Employed women	Housewives
			1972		
Job†	1	13.4*	17.9	16.8	16.0
	2,3	16.5	15.7	18.3	11.7
	4	23.0	23.3	21.0	25.5
	5,6	24.0	21.3	21.4	23.1
On own	7	23.0	21.8	22.5	23.8
	n	521	648	262	282
			1976		
Job	1	9.5	16.7	13.8	14.2
	2,3	15.3	16.6	15.9	15.7
	4	20.9	22.4	21.7	24.1
	5,6	29.9	24.3	28.7	25.8
On own	7	24.4	20.4	19.9	20.3
	n	815	977	428	345
			1980		
Job	1	11.9	11.3	6.9	15.7
	2,3	17.4	20.4	23.0	21.1
	4	17.8	23.6	23.3	20.5
	5,6	37.4	32.7	35.2	28.9
On own	7	15.6	11.9	11.6	13.9
	n	540	636	318	166

*All entries are percentages. Columns may not sum to 100 because of rounding.
†1 = Government see to a job and good standard of living.
  7 = Government let each person get ahead on own.

Questions about governmental concern over jobs and standards of living and government help for minorities were also asked in 1972 and 1976. Tables 2.24 and 2.25 show the results (all respondents, rather than just voters, are shown for purposes of comparison).

TABLE 2.25
Government Help for Minorities: 1972-1980

		Total men	Total women	Employed women	Housewives
			1972		
Help†	1	12.0*	14.7	16.1	9.8
	2,3	21.7	19.7	23.9	15.7
	4	23.5	23.5	23.3	24.7
	5,6	24.4	23.4	23.0	25.7
Not help	7	18.5	18.9	13.7	24.1
	n	882	1117	447	502
			1976		
Help	1	9.5	14.6	13.0	9.5
	2,3	23.2	20.7	22.3	17.2
	4	19.4	23.7	25.2	25.5
	5,6	25.8	21.1	22.7	23.7
Not help	7	22.1	20.1	16.8	24.0
	n	823	1029	476	337
			1980		
Help	1	4.5	5.8	4.0	4.8
	2,3	16.8	16.3	17.9	11.5
	4	27.6	31.2	31.2	32.5
	5,6	35.7	33.3	34.0	35.5
Not Help	7	15.5	13.4	13.0	15.7
	n	530	670	353	166

*All entries are percentages. Columns may not sum to 100 because of rounding.
†1 = Government should help minority groups. 7 = Minority groups should help themselves.

These tables considerably clarify the nature of public attitudes in 1980. Attitudes on the government's assuring jobs have not changed since 1972. The trend appears to be toward a moderation between both extremes on the issue. The percentages at 1, 2, and 3 and 5, 6, and 7 are about the same for all three years. The change in public attitudes toward government action to help minorities, however, is quite dramatic. In 1972 and 1976, the distribution was about the same. In 1980, support for government aid to minorities dropped dramatically—down 11 percent among men and 13 percent among employed women. Although there was movement away from the most anti position, the drop in support is undeniably large.

What Reagan was apparently in tune with was a set of antiwelfare, antifood stamp, antiminority, and prodefense attitudes among the general (i.e., white) public—*not* antigovernment attitudes per se. These attitudes, plus the general perception that the Democratic party had run out of workable ideas, go a long way toward explaining the popularity of Reagan's 1981 program—large tax cuts, deep reductions in social welfare programs (except, of course, for Social Security), and large increases for the military. They also explain why, after the apparent failure of supply-side economics in 1982, the public still supported Reagan and was willing to give his policies more time to work.[15]

The New Right, epitomized by the Moral Majority, had their own interpretation of Ronald Reagan's mandate. Their role in helping defeat many liberal Senate Democrats in 1978 and 1980 lent credibility to their claim that the 1980 victory of Ronald Reagan was a mandate for the traditional family (antifeminism), school prayer, and human life (antiabortion). Abortion was viewed as an important issue, especially by women, but it and school prayer did not differentiate Carter and Reagan voters. These issues did, however, differentiate Anderson from *both* Reagan and Carter voters. The Anderson voters can be characterized as being *strongly anti-Moral Majority*. Anderson voters opposed school prayer, did not think the Bible was literally true, and were strongly proabortion. Carter's fundamentalism was a handicap for him on these issues—it prevented him from gaining the support that Anderson drained away.

There was no mandate for Reagan *or anyone* on abortion. The abortion question asked in the 1980 postelection survey was also asked in 1972 and 1976. Table 2.26 shows the results. There is a clear

TABLE 2.26
Abortion: 1972-1980

		Total men	Total women	Employed women	Housewives
			1972		
Restrictive†	1	10.5*	11.7	7.5	15.2
	2	45.3	48.3	47.3	49.2
	3	18.1	16.7	19.5	14.4
Permissive	4	26.2	23.2	25.8	21.2
	n	1124	1493	586	693
			1976		
Restrictive	1	10.3	11.6	7.7	12.4
	2	41.9	47.1	41.6	52.5
	3	17.5	15.2	15.4	15.4
Permissive	4	28.8	24.9	33.9	18.4
	n	756	1086	454	402
			1980		
Restrictive	1	9.1	10.2	9.4	12.5
	2	44.9	44.5	40.4	51.0
	3	21.1	15.7	17.5	12.0
Permissive	4	24.9	29.6	32.8	24.5
	n	582	777	384	208

*All entries are percentages. Columns may not sum to 100 because of rounding.
†1 = Abortion should never be permitted.
2 = Abortion should be permitted only if the life and health of the woman is in danger.
3 = Abortion should be permitted if, due to personal reasons, the woman would have difficulty in caring for the child.
4 = Abortion should never be forbidden, since one should not require a woman to have a child she doesn't want.

trend in support for the *pro*abortion position—*especially among women*. Although a majority of men and women oppose abortion, the wording can have dramatic effect upon the distribution of attitudes. The 1980 preelection question, which omits the word "child" but mentions rape and incest as reasons to permit abortion, shows a majority supporting abortion. Only about 10 percent of the public are true hardliners who would never permit abortion under any circumstances. At the other extreme, about a third of the public, with women more supportive than men (about a 5 percent gap), would permit abortion without any restriction. Employed women are the most proabortion, men lean toward restriction, and housewives have the most restrictive attitude. Nevertheless, as Table 2.26 shows, the housewives' attitudes are shifting in favor of abortion. Because this issue is sensitive to wording, these numbers can be interpreted in many different ways. However, there is no way they can be interpreted as a mandate for a constitutional amendment to outlaw abortion.

Reagan's mandate was for a sharp cutback in all government spending except defense,* and for a large tax cut. In the touchy social issues area, only on school prayer do Reagan and his New Right followers have unambiguous support for their position. In total, Reagan's victory gave him a limited, but very significant, mandate.

On the negative side, Reagan's victory was as much a rejection of Jimmy Carter as it was a mandate for reducing spending and taxes. Carter, to put it mildly, was not a very popular man in November 1980. The issues on which a majority (or plurality) favored Carter's position did not work to his advantage. On the key issue of the election, government spending, a clear plurality favored *not* reducing spending. Yet, Carter was unable to get these people to vote for him at anything approaching the rates that those who favored *reducing* government spending voted for Reagan. The same pattern occurs on the key issue of a tax cut. Over 38 percent of those who favored *no* tax cut voted for Reagan. In sum, Carter was so unpopular that even people who agreed with him had difficulty voting for him. Reagan's victory was both a mandate and a rejection of Carter.

---

*And Social Security as it later turned out—Reagan evidently forgot Barry Goldwater's mistake on that issue in 1964.

GENDER AND THE VOTE IN 1980

1980 was the first presidential election in recent times in which the major candidates took clearly opposing views on issues affecting women. How much impact this had upon the outcome is not clear. Women and men differed sharply on the importance of abortion and equal-role issues, yet these two issues *did not* work in Carter's favor. Employed women thought that the equal-role issue was especially important (as important as tax cuts, abortion, and government spending, and slightly less important than defense spending) but they did not translate that into support for Carter. Even on the much debated Equal Rights Amendment—which both genders supported—employed women, the most supportive group, did not show strong support for Carter.

Although women and men differed about the importance of the issues affecting women, men did not necessarily differ sharply from women in their attitudes on these issues. On abortion for example, men, employed women, and housewives differed significantly in their distributions across the issue. But those differences are small compared to the distributions across the nuclear power issue, which apparently had no impact on the election whatsoever. All three groups had basically the same attitudes on the ERA. Men and employed women were similar in their attitudes toward discrimination against women. Sixty-five percent of employed women and 60 percent of men agree that society discriminates against women, while only 50 percent of housewives agree. For all women the figure is 60 percent—the same for all men.

The discrimination question shows the same pattern of support that we discussed in Chapter 1. Employed women care more intensely about issues affecting them as women than either men or housewives. Yet, when the support/approve categories are combined, employed women typically lead men by 5 or 7 percentage points. Does this constitute a women's vote? We think it is too early to tell.

BEYOND THE GENDER GAP

It is often said that public opinion follows public policy rather than the reverse. In the case of Ronald Reagan, we are given an unusual opportunity to test this truism. He was in many cases quite willing to compromise, but his public rhetoric was harsh. Whatever he did, he *said* he was embarking on a revolution. Our evidence suggests that by 1982 Reagan was both gaining adherents and losing them—on some questions, the public was coming around to his point of view and on others it was not. In this section we will use a large sample—not restricted to voters—since turnout in congressional elections is far less than turnout in presidential ones.

The discussion is incomplete because all questions used prior to 1980 were not included in subsequent surveys. Still, there is much that can be learned. We will discuss first those issues where the public adheres to Reagan. We then note those issues where Reagan is out of touch, and conclude with an assessment of the gender gap beyond 1980.

By 1982 virtually no one in either party was arguing for the traditional liberal solution of throwing money at problems. The Democratic leadership in the House and the Republican leadership in the Senate agreed with Reagan that things had gotten out of hand. Reagan's impressive victories in taxing and spending attest to this fact. Perhaps because the message was clear—enough is enough—mass opinion shifted substantially in Reagan's favor. On government spending, the shifts away from the "don't reduce government spending" end of the scale were substantial for all groups (see Table 2.27). There was not the positive thrust that Reagan had hoped for—there was not much regrouping at the "reduce" end of the scale. Rather, there was a drifting toward the center, away from the extreme liberal position. Among all groups the pattern was quite comparable; the "big spenders" were only about half as numerous as they were in 1980. On this issue then, Reagan was successful in changing the public's expectations of government.

But that is the sole example of opinion shifting in Reagan's direction. On other issues, such as the government's obligation to provide jobs and the question of abortion, 1982 produced no changes: Attitudes were just about the same as they were in 1980, and they were generally in the direction of the policy Reagan was pursuing. By and large, women and men in 1982 still wanted a reduced role for the federal government. 1980 seemed to be a watershed on such questions. Ironically, just as the percentage of social Darwinists (those who thought government should let each person get ahead on their own) declined from 22 percent in 1972 to

TABLE 2.27
Government Spending: 1980-1982

		Total men	Total women	Employed women	Housewives
			1980		
Reduce†	1	8.5*	8.0	6.6	9.8
	2,3	30.0	22.1	23.6	23.6
	4	17.1	21.8	21.8	21.3
	5,6	27.2	28.4	31.0	25.3
Don't reduce	7	17.2	19.7	17.1	20.1
	n	580	725	381	174
			1982		
Reduce	1	13.0	8.8	6.6	14.2
	2,3	34.5	25.5	27.7	25.3
	4	26.3	30.7	30.1	32.7
	5,6	19.2	24.3	26.6	19.1
Don't reduce	7	7.1	10.8	9.0	8.6
	n	525	593	289	162

*All entries are percentages. Columns may not sum to 100 because of rounding.
†1 = Government should provide many fewer services; reduce spending a lot.
7 = Government should continue to provide services; no reduction in spending.

14 percent in 1980 and 1982, a president espousing such views was elected. There is still not much support for the other extreme (a government-guaranteed job), as the center continues to attract the greatest support.

There is, however, one issue about which the public has clearly abandoned the president: defense spending. Possibly because there were mixed messages here, with prominent members of the president's party arguing in favor of reducing defense expenditures while Reagan clung stubbornly to increasing them, the public by 1982 had lost its fascination with military hardware. Here the shifts in opinion are substantial. In 1980 only 11 percent of the respondents placed themselves at the "decrease" end of the defense spending scale (positions 1, 2, 3). By 1982 the percentage had increased to 35. The traditional difference between women and men over the use of force reemerged clearly in 1982 (see Table 2.28). The shift of employed women away from Reagan on this issue was much larger than the shift away by men. Any mandate Reagan had for his stupendous defense buildup had largely evaporated by 1982.

Given the fact that the gender gap has become a media event, one which—whatever its empirical validity—clearly troubles Reagan and excites Democrats, we need to know how much of a gap exists. In 1983, an aspirant for the Democratic nomination, Senator Gary Hart (D-Colo.), promised women's organizations that he would use

TABLE 2.28
Defense Spending: 1980-1982

		Total men	Total women	Employed women	Housewives
			1980		
Decrease†	1	2.7*	3.5	3.1	2.1
	2,3	7.0	9.0	10.9	7.9
	4	12.8	22.0	19.8	24.9
	5,6	52.6	43.6	43.8	43.4
Increase	7	24.9	21.9	22.4	21.7
	n	626	736	384	189
			1982		
Decrease	1	9.8	11.0	13.3	7.6
	2,3	21.4	27.8	29.8	26.4
	4	28.5	35.5	31.6	37.1
	5,6	34.3	21.7	21.4	25.2
Increase	7	6.0	4.1	3.9	3.8
	n	533	591	285	159

*All entries are percentages. Columns may not sum to 100 because of rounding.
†1 = Greatly decrease defense spending.
7 = Greatly increase defense spending.

the power of the presidency to coerce states—by granting and withholding federal funds—into adopting the ERA. Such a rash statement would surely not have been made if the reality of the gender gap were not widely accepted. The evidence is less conclusive. In the following tables we measure how differently distributed an indicated pair is (as was done in Table 2.8). The smaller the number, the more identical the distribution of the two groups across a scale. Table 2.29 shows four issues asked only in 1980 and 1982; Table 2.30 shows issues across a longer time period. At first glance, the gender gap appears real. Except for abortion, the gap increases between men and women. But at the same time, *the gap between employed women and housewives also increased.* On abortion and the ERA, the gap between employed women and housewives is greater than the gap between men and women. On government spending, the two gaps are only trivially different. On defense spending, a legitimate gender gap exists.

Looking at the gender gap over a longer period of time provides yet more evidence of its elusive nature. The government jobs issues provide a good example of consistently expanding gender gap, but issues of government help for minorities and an equal role for women do not. There is less of a gap on the minorities issue than there was in 1976. Issues of women's equal role do not produce a gender gap but reveals a major gap between employed women and housewives.

All in all, these data do not argue for a stable gender gap and reinforce our essential point: The difference *between* women is often as great as the gender gap, and in some cases greater.

None of this means, of course, that the widely reported distaste for Reagan among women does not exist. Nor does it mean that, in response to Reagan's obvious inability to communicate his alleged concern for women's rights, he will not continue to face female opposition.[16]

We do suggest, however, that there is not a stable gap. There does not need to be to justify the claim for a women's vote. It was widely assumed that women would translate hostility toward Reagan into support for the Democrats in the 1982 congressional elections. Preelection surveys to the contrary, this did not occur. There was a gap in 1982. Women at all education and income levels gave slight preference to the Democrats: Still, a male-female difference of between three and six points does not suggest much more than irritation. This election is not a fair comparison, as Reagan was not

TABLE 2.29
The Gender Gap: 1980-1982

	Government spending		Defense spending		Abortion		ERA*	
	1980	1982	1980	1982	1980	1982	1980	1982
Men/women	8.4†	13.2	12.0	14.6	4.4	3.8	2.5	11.7
Men/employed women	8.5	13.2	11.3	15.0	5.9	6.7	3.5	12.4
Men/housewives	8.4	9.2	13.0	13.6	12.9	13.4	1.8	14.5
Employed women/housewives	6.2	10.3	5.1	9.3	16.2	16.8	4.0	14.2

†The mean of the sum of the absolute values of the differences between the percentages of the two groups at the various scale positions divided by the maximum possible mean absolute percentage difference. Maximum possible value is 100.
*Question not identically worded in 1980 and 1982.

TABLE 2.30
The Gender Gap: 1972-1982

	1972	1976	1980	1982
	\multicolumn{4}{c}{Government jobs and standard of living}			
Men/women	4.8	9.8	8.9	13.6
Men/employed women	5.2	5.7	11.2	10.3
Men/housewives	5.8	8.3	10.2	12.0
Employed women/housewives	7.5	3.2	11.1	8.2
	\multicolumn{4}{c}{Government help for minorities}			
Men/women	3.1	9.3	5.0	6.1
Men/employed women	6.4	9.3	4.7	8.1
Men/housewives	8.2	8.1	5.5	7.5
Employed women/housewives	14.5	8.6	6.4	7.7
	\multicolumn{4}{c}{Equal role for women}			
Men/women	7.0	4.5	5.4	6.4
Men/employed women	11.0	5.5	8.1	9.7
Men/housewives	13.5	22.0	9.3	15.4
Employed women/housewives	18.5	26.5	16.1	22.6

running. Frankovic calls our attention to the fact that women view Reagan more negatively than men do. "Whenever Ronald Reagan's name is mentioned in a survey question there are significant sex differences."[17]

Beyond Reagan, beyond the infamous gender gap, can there be a women's vote? Sapiro addresses the question by examining the reasons for expecting differences between the sexes to remain relatively minor, and then by proposing reasons to expect them to enlarge. Most of these reasons have been discussed in this book: Women will not be different from men because they do not differ significantly in their lifestyle. Nevertheless, there should be emerging differences because women are becoming more politically sophisticated and more likely to use gender as a focus of self-identification.[18]

Given the pluses and minuses, it is probable that a women's vote will not develop in the same way that Jewish or black votes have. Rather than being counted upon to stay reasonably loyal across the board, women may respond to *specific* candidates and events in a cohesive manner. Beyond this situational response, the electoral process will not yield a women's point of view. The expectation is unrealistic. Just as the commonly held views about the greater pacifism of women are not completely accurate,[19] and reports of a gender gap exaggerated, so are hopes for an increase in the power of gender in predicting attitude. Gender interacts in complex ways with other variables, only a few of which are analyzed and understood.

NOTES

1. Women are always overrepresented in these cross-sectional surveys because they are home more often when the interviewer calls.

2. In 1982, gender differences in turnout were trivial. See Virginia Sapiro, "Women, Political Action, and Political Participation," *American Political Science Review* 77 (June 1983): 28. Also see Chapter 4 in this text.

3. On the decline of these ideas see John Stucker, "Women as Voters: Their Maturation as Political Persons in American Society," in M. Githens and J. Prestage, Eds., *A Portrait of Marginality. The Political Behavior of American Women* (New York: Longman, 1977), pp. 264-283.

4. On the related question of party identification, Baxter and Lansing conclude that "there was a remarkable similarity among women and men stating their preference for political party." In Sandra Baxter and Marjorie Lansing, *Women and Politics* (Ann Arbor: University of Michigan Press, 1980), p. 67.

5. In particular see the 1981 NOW pamplet, "Women Can Make the Difference."

6. *Public Opinion,* December/January 1983, p. 34.

7. *Public Opinion,* December/January 1983, p. 38.

8. *Public Opinion,* April/May 1982, pp. 21-32.

9. Kristi Andersen, "Working Women and Political Participation," *American Journal of Political Science 19* (August 1975): 452.

10. The numbers in Table 2.10 are arrived at by taking the mean of the sum of the absolute values of the differences between the Carter and Reagan voter percentages at the various scale positions (for the relevant groups) and dividing this number by the maximum possible mean absolute percentage difference so scales with different numbers of points are comparable. (This, in effect, results in a division by 200.)

11. Baxter and Lansing, *Women and Politics*, p. 57.

12. Baxter and Lansing, *Women and Politics*, p. 59. Similar conclusions are reached by Kathleen A. Frankovic, "Sex and Politics—New Alignments, Old Issues." *Political Science* (Summer 1982) 445.

13. *Gallup Poll Index,* March 1964, p. 8.

14. Our findings here are consistent with those of Frankovic, "Sex and Politics," p. 445.

15. A poll taken in July 1982 by Richard Wirthlin, President Reagan's pollster, showed that 54 percent supported Reagan's economic program and 60 percent felt it would take another year to work. An earlier poll by CBS/*New York Times* generally supported these findings. See the 31 July 1982 edition of the *New York Times*, p. 8.

16. See "The Gender Gap: No Presidential Candidate Can Afford to Write Off the Nation's Largest Bloc of Voters," *National Journal 15* (29 October 1983): 2204-2205.

17. Frankovic, "Sex and Politics," p. 441.

18. Sapiro, "Women, Political Action, and Political Participation," pp. 34-35.

19. Sapiro, *The Political Integration of Women* (Urbana, Ill.: University of Illinois Press, 1983), p. 166.

3
Ideology and the Attitudes of Women in 1980

INTRODUCTION

If 1980 was not a referendum on conservatism, does this mean that Americans are not ideological? Many people make this argument: Americans are *pragmatic;* they look for solutions, not causes. They migrate toward the middle of the road, avoiding extremes of left and right. We believe the vital center surely exists, but that does not mean that people cannot tell you whether they are liberals, moderates, or conservatives. If people gave random answers to questions of ideological orientation then responses over time would show no pattern. This is not the case.

Beginning in 1972, the ICPSR at the University of Michigan began asking respondents to place themselves on a liberal/conservative seven-point scale. The seven points were labelled as follows: extremely liberal, liberal, slightly liberal, moderate/middle of the road, slightly conservative, conservative, and extremely conservative. We categorized respondents as "liberal" if they placed themselves at points 1, 2, or 3; as "moderate" if they placed themselves at point 4; as "conservative" if they placed themselves at points 5, 6, or 7.

The words "liberal," "conservative," and "ideological" have become mixed together in American political discourse. Ever since the New Deal, the labels liberal and conservative have concerned government intervention in the economy—the fundamental basis of conflict in American politics. Liberals have favored government intervention in the economy to ameliorate the effects of capitalism on the lower social classes, while conservatives have opposed such intervention, arguing that free enterprise, if left alone, will in the end make everyone better off. Ideology, which we used in its generic sense in Chapter 1 (ideology *qua* belief system), came to mean liberal/conservative in the above sense. However, ever since the social turmoil of the 1960s, liberal and conservative have acquired new shades of meaning. Liberal and conservative are now connected to attitudes on issues that concern the extent to which government intrudes into the private lives of individuals. The most salient issue of this type is abortion. Other examples are homosexuality, marijuana, and, most recently, the treatment of deformed newborn infants. Conservatives such as President Reagan favor government intervention into the private lives of individuals on these issues while liberals oppose such government intervention.

These issues, along with school prayer, equal rights for women, school busing, aiding minority groups, and similar problems can be loosely grouped as *social issues*.[1] Issues involving women and minority groups concern the extent to which government will intervene to promote their civil rights—to alter the status quo in favor of the affected group. Liberals favor the expansion of the civil rights of groups that have been (for whatever reasons) discriminated against both economically and socially, while conservatives oppose such expansion.

The common thread running through these social issues is government action or inaction to expand the rights of individuals or groups. On some issues, such as deformed infant treatment, *conservatives* are trying to *change* the status quo and *restrict* the traditional right of the parents, in conjunction with their physician, to determine treatment. On issues concerning discrimination against women, *liberals* want the government to take action to *change* the status quo to *expand* the rights of women.

For the most part, attitudes on economic and social issues are related. Liberals favor government intervention in the economy and favor government intervention to expand the rights of individuals and groups. Conservatives oppose government intervention in the economy and oppose government intervention to expand the rights of individuals and groups. This is particularly true of active politicians and less true of the mass public. As we saw in Chapter 2, abortion played almost no role in the 1980 election in terms of helping or hurting either candidate, whereas other issues affecting women—which for the most part are social issues—did play a role.

One of the by-products of the conflict over the Equal Rights Amendment appears to be the movement of women's issues from noncontroversial to the social issue category. In 1976 the correlations between the women's liberation movement feeling thermometer and the feeling thermometers for Carter and Ford were .143 and −.005, respectively, indicating that attitudes toward women's liberation played almost no role in evaluating the presidential candidates. Breaking the correlations down by gender category produced no significant differences. In 1980, however, the correlations between the women's liberation movement feeling thermometer and the Carter, Reagan, Kennedy, and Anderson thermometers were .241, .177, .327, and .240, respectively. Clearly, attitudes toward the women's liberation movement in 1980 had a much greater impact upon candidate evaluation.

A factor analysis of the correlation matrices between the issue scales for the gender categories confirms the increasing dissension about women's issues since 1972. For example, a factor analysis of the correlation matrix computed between 14 issue scales and the four major presidential candidates (Carter, Reagan, Kennedy, Anderson) feeling thermometers revealed two primary dimensions underlying the correlations. The pre- and postelection liberal/conservative seven-point scales, the pre- and postelection strength of party identification seven-point scale, the government aid to minorities seven-point scale, the government-guaranteed job and good standard of living seven-point scale, the inflation seven-point scale, the government spending seven-point scale, and the Carter, Kennedy, and Reagan feeling thermometers all load on the first dimension. This dimension is clearly the New Deal government intervention in the economy dimension. The pre- and postelection four-point abortion scale questions and the equal role for women seven-point scale load on the second dimension. The John Anderson and women's liberation movement feeling thermometer, the relations with the U.S.S.R. seven-point scale, and the defense spending seven-point scale all load equally on the two dimensions. Loadings on higher dimensions are insignificant.

If we confined ourselves to looking at only the 1980 issue correlations, we could conclude only that the second dimension was picking up only those issues, like abortion and defense spending, which *cut across party lines.* Abortion and an equal role for women tap the basic issue of government intervention to promote the civil rights of individuals and groups, but attitudes toward the U.S.S.R. and defense spending do not. In 1972 and 1976, however, more social issue questions—for example, attitudes about the rights of accused criminals, marijuana, student demonstrations, how to deal with urban rioters—were asked. These issues, along with the abortion and women's equal-role scales, loaded highly on the second dimension. The weight of the evidence is that the second dimension underlying the issue scale correlations is the basic issue of government intervention to promote the civil rights of individuals and groups. When politicians like John Anderson and issues like relations with the U.S.S.R. appear and cut across party lines, they tend to load on the social issues dimension because of the shared characteristic of party line blurring.

For the remainder of this chapter, when we use the word *ideology* we mean liberal/conservative in the two senses just discussed. As we noted above, the liberal/conservative seven-point scale appears to tap people's attitudes primarily on government intervention in the economy. The mass public thus seems to understand the words liberal and conservative in their New Deal context. This is shown by the high correlations between the liberal/conservative scale, the strength of party identification scale, and the feeling thermometers for the major party candidates. These correlations are all around .4 in magnitude—which is quite high given the ordinal character of the data. Given that the liberal/conservative scale for the sample as a whole is primarily tapping the economic aspect of ideology as we have defined it, we can use the scale to analyze and classify the substantive issues in the 1980 election by our gender categories. We will show that breaking the respondents down by gender reveals that some groups understand the term liberal differently from others.

IDEOLOGY AND WOMEN'S ISSUES

An Equal Role for Women

The place to begin our issue analysis is with the women's equal-role seven-point scale which we analyzed extensively in Chapter 1.

Overall, the liberal/conservative scale, is, as expected, only weakly related to attitudes on an equal role for women. However, dividing the respondents by gender shows a different story. Three-fourths of all employed women who claim to be liberal also score at the highest point on the equal role for women scale (see Table 3.1). Only 36 percent of liberal housewives do so. Liberal housewives, are not, however, entirely opposed to equal rights for women, choosing instead the position just beneath the top. To them, being a liberal does not mean absolute equality, while for employed women, it does. Conversely, conservative employed women do not believe a woman's place is in the home. They too adopt the more moderate position. Conservative employed women are just about as egalitarian as liberal housewives.

Table 3.1 shows that in 1980 the overall weak relationship between the two scales is due to the men. For them, liberalism is, in effect, unrelated to attitudes about equality. In terms of the typology we laid out in Chapter 1, there is no *constraint* between self-identified liberalism/conservatism and attitudes on women's equality for men.

The correlation between the two scales for men is only .13, while for housewives it is .35 and for employed women .25. Although these correlations are not large, it does appear that when women use the terms liberal and conservative they use them in a broader sense than men do.

TABLE 3.1

Distribution of Respondents on Equal-Role Scale by Ideology: 1980-1982 (Percent Choosing Equal Role)

	1980	1982	1980	1982
IDEOLOGY	Total Men		Total Women	
Liberal	46	65	65	63
Moderate	33	34	34	43
Conservative	31	26	29	36
	Employed women		Housewives	
Liberal	76	67	36	50
Moderate	42	49	26	28
Conservative	39	44	18	20

Constraint is, as we would expect, strongly related to education. Here we use only employed women, since housewives do not on the whole get as much education (hence, they cannot be compared at all educational levels). Liberalism and equality are more strongly related with each increment of education. In all three categories (high school, some college, college graduate), liberals are more egalitarian than conservatives, but the differences are more substantial as education increases. The percentage of conservative women who are strongly egalitarian changes very little with education: Education adds only about 6 percent to strong egalitarian feelings. Among liberal women, however, education adds about 38 percent of egalitarian sentiments. Thus the gap between liberals and conservatives is greatest among the college educated.

The three variables—liberalism, education, and job status—interact cumulatively: college-educated employed women who regard themselves as politically liberal are the most egalitarian group in the sample, with a resounding 88 percent selecting the first position on the equal-role scale. Are there any women left who still think they should stay home and stand by their man? Indeed there are: 21 percent of housewives who regard themselves as conservative and have only a high school education select scale position seven, the most traditional. Fifty-three percent of this group is below position five on the equal-role scale.[2]

But these attitudes are volatile. In a scant two years, constraint for men increased; the correlation improved to .28, due largely to the improving synchronization in attitude among the liberal men. They jumped up from 45.5 percent to 64.7 percent in their support for the most egalitarian response to the equal-role scale. In 1980, liberal men were conspicuously out of sync (compared to women, especially employed women). However, by 1982 they developed much more consistency. Why this is the case cannot be confirmed but we can speculate. Assuming that mass opinion follows elite cues, there was not much doubt that—in spite of Reagan's protestations—the Republican administration did not intend to carry on with a business-as-usual attitude toward women. Reagan sent out clear rhetorical signals that the high visibility women's programs were low on his priority list. Perhaps the liberal men were nudged up. Since conservative men became *less* egalitarian, the idea makes sense. The argument is confused a bit by changes in the attitudes of women. Liberal employed women became less egalitarian and conservative employed women became more egalitarian; but, among housewives, liberals became more egalitarian (and, strangely, located a bit more at the most traditional point on the scale). The result is a decrease in constraint among housewives. The net consequence of these changes is to blur the differences between women and men. By 1982, abstract ideology and egalitarianism were constrained to about the same degree in the three groups.

While there are more arguments to be examined about constraint, the fact that women become more consistent, if it proves to be more than a temporary phenomenon, becomes significant—especially if we consider the conclusions of previous research. Fulenwider asserts that "Feminism among women is more tightly structured than feminism among men. . . . Values are central to the content of feminism for women, while for men feminism is primarily a descriptive belief set. . . . The evidence is clear and strong. Feminism is a central and important belief set for women, a more peripheral one for men."[3]

Women's Liberation Movement

There is no necessary reason why liberalism in its economic sense should be related to attitudes toward people and organizations associated with the women's liberation movement. Presumably, when one mentions such organizations, those most active in espousing feminist goals come to mind. However, there are many

TABLE 3.2
Ideology and the Women's Liberation Feeling Thermometer

		Employed women			Housewives		
		Liberal	Moderate	Conservative	Liberal	Moderate	Conservative
Cold	0-20	3.9*	10.0	20.2	-	11.6	19.6
	21-40	1.9	16.4	18.2	18.2	25.6	23.5
	41-60	23.1	41.8	27.3	40.9	32.6	37.3
	61-80	23.1	20.0	20.2	18.2	16.3	11.8
Warm	81-100	48.1	11.8	14.1	22.7	14.0	7.8
	n	52	110	99	22	43	51

*All entries are percentages. Columns may not sum to 100 because of rounding.

different kinds of organizations. The profeminist ones range from radical to mainstream. And, of course, Phyllis Schlafly's organization led the counterattack. The linkage between the thermometer and the liberal/conservative scale is stronger than was the case for liberalism and belief in equality. Table 3.2 shows that liberal employed women are those with the most positive attitude toward women's organizations. Liberal housewives are far less warm toward them. These facts are reflected in the correlations between the two scales. The correlation between the women's liberation movement feeling thermometer and the liberal/conservative seven-point scale was −.35 for employed women and a somewhat weaker −.26 for both housewives and men in 1980.

Employed women show some surprising patterns. As anticipated, Table 3.3 shows that position on the feeling thermometer is directly related to education, with the college-educated groups more than twice as warm as the lesser educated women. But note the surprising support for women's liberation among lesser educated conservative women. A hefty minority of conservative employed women are warm toward women's liberation.

The fact that employed women are distinctly different from men and housewives in their coupling of self-identified liberalism and their attitudes on women's liberation makes a great deal of sense. Employed women are exposed daily to inequities in the workplace. Housewives have no such exposure. As a consequence, employed women are far more likely, *ceteris paribus,* to become aware of women's organizations that seek to implement feminist goals. Since implementing equality in the workplace almost certainly entails some form of government intervention, it is not surprising that the correlation between liberalism and the women's liberation movement thermometer is quite high.

Much the same information is found by examining party identification—although the relationship is somewhat weaker. Democrats, whether employed women or housewives, are warmer (although only 22 percent are at the highest point on the thermometer). Among employed women, college-educated Democrats are warmest (but only 45 percent are at the top of the thermometer). The correlations between the women's liberation thermometer and party identification are all very close to −.16. There is very little variation in the correlation across the gender categories. Although we found in the factor analysis that party identification and

TABLE 3.3
Ideology, Women's Liberation Thermometer, and Education

		Liberal	Moderate	Conservative
			Employed women: high school	
Cold	0-20	15.4*	12.9	27.9
	21-40	7.7	20.2	14.0
	41-60	38.5	33.9	27.9
	61-80	15.4	19.4	16.3
Warm	81-100	23.1	12.9	14.0
	n	13	62	43
			Employed: some college	
Cold	0-20	-	7.1	22.2
	21-40	-	14.3	11.1
	41-60	30.8	46.4	25.9
	61-80	15.4	25.0	33.3
Warm	81-100	53.9	7.1	7.4
	n	13	28	27
			Employed: college	
Cold	0-20	-	5.0	6.9
	21-40	-	5.0	31.0
	41-60	11.5	60.0	27.6
	61-80	30.8	15.0	13.8
Warm	81-100	57.7	15.0	20.7
	n	26	20	29

*All entries are percentages. Columns may not sum to 100 because of rounding.

liberalism both loaded significantly only on the government-in-the-economy dimension, the correlations between the two were only about .4 for all groups. These are high correlations given the ordinal character of the scales, but the two are by no means measuring the same thing.

Discrimination Against Women

A problem for emergent groups is their ability to persuade their potential clientele that there is need for their services. People may be attracted to a group because it provides professional opportunities, personal benefits (cheap insurance, charter flights, etc.), or social opportunities. They may also belong because they believe in the political goals of the group. Women's groups, as we have seen, are not universally popular even among their natural clientele. Most women's organizations offer little in the way of selective benefits; they only offer relief from discrimination.

Thus early stages of the development of the women's movement featured consciousness raising sessions. The goal was to get women to understand that they had a problem, no easy task at the time. Old patterns of submission die hard, but they do die. Table 3.4 shows that there is a robust relationship between liberalism and the belief that society discriminates against women, both among employed women and housewives. Majorities of liberals in both groups strongly agree that society discriminates against women. Indeed, substantial minorities of the conservatives agree strongly.

Whether or not the belief in discrimination is enough to fuel a social movement is not clear. The fact that belief in discrimination is linked to liberalism is, while not astonishing, troublesome. Conservative housewives who do not think society discriminates against women also feel that a woman's place is in the home. They are consistent in the sense we discussed in Chapter 1. That is, there is a high degree of constraint present in their attitudes. Conservative employed women who do *not* think society discriminates against women are *not* consistent however. Two-thirds of them feel that men and women should have an equal role (our egalitarian category). Do conservative employed women actually experience less discrimination, or do they ignore it?

Using education as a control provides some further information. Among high-school educated employed women, liberalism is of little consequence in predicting whether or not a woman believes society discriminates against women. Ideology makes its impact among the better educated. Here liberalism and belief in discrimination are strongly related. Since the women in Table 3.3 are all employed, they all have approximately the same risk of discrimination. Even so, liberals are more troubled. Perhaps liberals are more bothered by discrimination because they have higher expectations. Yet among college-educated employed women, even the conservatives (53 percent) report that society discriminates against women. A reasonable conclusion is that, albeit with substantial variation, women have gotten the message: Discrimination is not just a myth cooked up to radicalize them. It is real.

But what about men? There is a lot of emotion involved here. Men have frequently been portrayed as more sympathetic to feminist goals than women. Their generally favorable opinions on, for example, the Equal Rights Amendment are cited as evidence. Table 3.4 shows, however, that a partial explanation for their feminist sympathies is that they are less sensitive to the existence of discrimination!

Much like blacks' and whites' views about racial discrimination (whites are less likely to acknowledge discrimination than are blacks), men *irrespective of liberalism or education,* are inclined to agree that society discriminates against women less than women do. Men are as they have been described by feminist leaders—insensitive. Liberal men are more sensitive than conservative men, but far less sensitive than liberal women.

TABLE 3.4
Ideology and Discrimination Against Women: 1980

	Liberal	Moderate	Conservative	Liberal	Moderate	Conservative
	Total Men			Total Women		
Strongly agree†	43.3*	34.2	29.2	66.0	34.9	31.9
Agree	33.3	26.7	29.7	15.5	27.4	25.7
Disagree	11.1	25.0	17.3	9.3	24.1	22.5
Strongly disagree	12.2	14.2	23.9	9.3	13.7	19.9
n	90	120	226	97	212	191
	Employed women			Housewives		
Strongly agree	69.2	47.7	38.2	59.1	23.9	29.4
Agree	13.5	23.4	24.5	22.7	19.6	23.5
Disagree	9.6	15.9	25.5	9.1	43.5	17.7
Strongly disagree	7.7	13.1	11.8	9.1	13.0	29.4
n	52	107	102	22	46	51

*All entries are percentages. Columns may not sum to 100 because of rounding.
†Are women discriminated against in society?

Abortion

If ever an issue cut broad swaths across the liberal/conservative economic dichotomy, abortion is it. Surely the most explosive issue of our day, it has generated scores of single issue groups for and against it. Since the landmark *Roe* vs. *Wade* Supreme Court decision legalizing abortion, federal funds have been granted for abortion and then denied. Feelings run so high that conservative members of Congress are trying to write legislation specifying the fetus as a human being, thus guaranteeing First Amendment rights. President Reagan, in a significant gesture toward the New Right, supports an antiabortion constitutional amendment. This issue divides liberals and conservatives, housewives and employed women, with stark clarity. Table 3.5 shows that employed women tend to favor unrestricted abortion; housewives less so. Seventy-eight percent of liberal employed women want unrestricted abortion, but only 41 percent of liberal housewives do. Conservative women, whether they are housewives or employed, do not want unrestricted abortion. Conservative employed women, *irrespective of their education,* do not want unrestricted abortion. But among liberal women, employed or housewives, education is strongly predictive in the link between liberalism and abortion. Among liberals, the percentages favoring unrestricted abortion almost double between the least and most educated groups. An astonishing 96 percent of liberal employed women with a college education favor unrestricted abortion. If a person is a conservative, then gender and education have no effect on attitudes toward abortion. Just the opposite is true of liberals.

TABLE 3.5
Ideology and Abortion: 1980-1982 (Percentage of Liberals Preferring the Most Permissive Abortion Option)

	1980	1982
Total men	51	66
Total women	68	53
Employed women	78	66
Housewives	55	50

Thus the issue of abortion produces both consensus and conflict. However, there is virtually *no* support for the absolutist antiabortion position. Very few want to forbid abortions under any circumstances. Even among conservative housewives and poorly educated conservative employed women, the extreme position finds almost no support. Furthermore, substantial minorities of these groups (about 35 percent) favor a more permissive policy.

The consensus is that some abortions should be permitted some of the time. Except for liberal employed women (who at every educational level muster a majority for the most permissive position), women are divided. The balance seems to be somewhat more toward the restrictive end of the spectrum: Moderate and conservative housewives and employed women are bunched up toward the top. Excluding the liberal employed women, who favor unrestricted abortion, the moderates and conservatives with less than a college education also cluster toward the top of the scale. Even among the college graduates, there is no consensus. The balance of opinion seems to be that abortion should be permitted only if the life and the health of the woman is in danger. When abortions are permitted, they are not at the whim of the mother-to-be. Rather, with the exception of the liberal employed women, abortions are viewed as serious decisions permitted only under conditions of apparent danger.

The Equal Rights Amendment

The now defunct Equal Rights Amendment yields substantially more consensus, and was more obviously linked to liberalism. Liberals were for it; conservatives were not (see Table 3.6). Among liberals, employed women were for it (75 percent) more than housewives (62 percent) or men (58 percent). Among liberal employed women, college graduates were more enthusiastic (81 percent) than those with only some college (76 percent) or with high school educations (58 percent). In short, anybody who claimed to be a liberal was for it; they varied only in degree of enthusiasm. Conversely, anybody who claimed to be a conservative was against it.

The ERA will no doubt ultimately be resubmitted continuously for ratification. Therefore, we should keep in mind that it, like other women's issues, has the same general clientele: liberal, college-educated employed women. From the welter of patterns we

TABLE 3.6
The Equal Rights Amendment: 1980

		Liberal	Moderate	Conservative	Liberal	Moderate	Conservative
			Total men			Total women	
Approve†	1	58.0*	24.6	23.6	69.9	28.2	19.1
	2	27.3	34.6	21.2	23.7	36.2	25.1
	3	9.1	23.6	21.2	4.3	18.6	21.3
Disapprove	4	5.7	17.3	34.0	2.2	17.0	34.4
	n	88	110	212	93	188	183
			Employed women			Housewives	
Approve	1	74.5	31.3	15.3	61.9	15.0	23.4
	2	19.6	35.4	30.6	28.6	45.0	19.2
	3	2.0	16.7	22.5	9.5	17.5	19.2
Disapprove	4	3.9	16.7	31.6	-	22.5	38.3
	n	51	96	98	21	40	47

*All entries are percentages. Columns may not sum to 100 because of rounding.
†1 = Strongly approve the Equal Rights Amendment.
2 = Not strongly approve.
3 = Not strongly disapprove.
4 = Strongly disapprove.

identified in the responses to issues affecting women, this pattern emerges consistently and with great clarity: Liberal employed women mean something different by liberal than do the other groups. For them, being liberal means, as we shall see below, government intervention in the economy as well as government intervention on behalf of equal rights for women—to eliminate discrimination, to allow safe abortions, to pass the Equal Rights Amendment. Conservatives, regardless of gender, and liberal men and housewives do not display this consistency.

The Equal Rights Amendment was a key issue differentiating preference for Carter and Reagan and, despite its present position in limbo, will return to the public agenda. The emotionalism of the response to the defeat of the ERA is well illustrated by the strong relationship between ideology and the reaction to that defeat. Conservatives were delirious with joy, while liberals were understandably dismayed (see Table 3.7). Conservative men were apparently only paying lip service to the ERA in 1980. They supported it more than conservative women, but were more pleased at its defeat. Much of the speculation about the shallowness of male support for ERA is, alas, at least reinforced, if not confirmed. The keen disappointment showed up in our previous discussion of the gender gap in Chapter 2; there was a big jump in this gap measure between 1980 and 1982.[4]

TABLE 3.7
The Equal Rights Amendment: 1982

		Liberal	Moderate	Conservative	Liberal	Moderate	Conservative
			Total men			Total women	
Pleased it	1	9.4*	12.7	41.3	7.9	15.7	30.7
failed†	2	12.5	25.4	20.3	9.0	15.7	31.5
	3	37.5	50.7	24.8	31.5	36.0	22.8
Disappointed	4	40.6	11.3	3.7	51.7	32.6	15.0
	n	64	71	109	89	89	127
			Employed women			Housewives	
Pleased it	1	8.2	12.0	28.4	12.5	30.0	37.5
failed†	2	6.1	14.0	31.3	12.5	15.0	30.0
	3	38.8	38.0	23.9	18.8	30.0	17.5
Disappointed	4	46.9	36.0	16.4	56.3	25.0	15.0
	n	49	50	67	16	20	40

All entries are percentages. Columns may not sum to 100 because of rounding.
1 = Very pleased ERA didn't pass.
2 = Somewhat pleased.
3 = Somewhat disappointed.
4 = Very disappointed.

OTHER ISSUES

Liberalism becomes less useful in characterizing women's attitudes. As we noted in the last chapter, women's responses to the issues in the 1980 campaign were not cohesive. We should expect, consequently, that liberal/conservative orientation is less likely to constrain specific attitudes than was the case with issues of particular salience to women—especially employed women. We begin with two issues of continuing interest, due to the forceful presentation of their agenda by the New Right, and the sometimes reluctant embrace of this agenda by President Reagan. The two issues are prayer in the schools and busing. Some predict that these issues will die away, but those familiar with the tenacity of the New Right doubt it. With President Reagan supporting a constitutional amendment allowing school prayer, and with local courts finding ingenious ways to frustrate the American Civil Liberties Union, these issues, trite though they may appear, will be with us for some time.

School Prayer

Employed liberal women stand apart on the school prayer issue, as they do on issues affecting women. They do not want prayers, whereas their liberal counterparts among housewives and men are evenly divided. The liberals are split, but the conservatives are not. All conservatives, male or female, want those prayers. The durability of this conservative belief is made apparent when the relationship between ideology and preference for school prayers among employed women is broken down by education. Conservatives, no matter what educational level, want prayers. Liberals do not, but only at the more advanced educational levels. There is not as much of a difference between the sexes as there is within them: Liberal women are the most *opposed* to prayers; conservative women are the most *in favor* of them. The only firm supporters of the separation of church and state are the liberal, relatively well-educated, employed women. An amendment to allow prayers would stand a good chance, if popular preferences were translated into public policy.

Busing

Having children pray in school is one thing; busing them there is quite another. Of all the items on the social agenda of the New Right, few have aroused so much antagonism on the part of the general public. Willingness to bus children is also a women's issue, since women have traditionally assumed more responsibility for education than men have. However, the women most likely to have their undivided attention directed to this issue, housewives, loathe the idea. Obviously, a willingness to support busing is related to liberalism. Liberals hate busing just a little bit less than conservatives. But conservative housewives hate it more than any other group. Although nobody really thinks busing is a swell idea, housewives appear ready to take to the barricades. Employed women, more progressive generally, are somewhat more tolerant. Even education takes less of a bite here. The highly educated employed women, traditionally our most liberal group, can best be described as least opposed to busing, since only 13 percent of them are actually enthusiastic.

Busing is, because of universal distaste, not vulnerable to liberalism as a predictor. Still, there are extremes. The most antibusing type is a conservative housewife with a high school education.

Helping Minorities

Busing was instigated to help minorities. However, opposition to busing really has very little to do with whether or not a person believes in uplifting the downtrodden. A more direct question—should the government aid minorities—is better. Given assumptions about the compassion of women, we might expect them to be more inclined to help the less fortunate. To a limited degree, they are. Although few select the most extreme response, liberal employed women cluster just beneath the top of the seven-point scale. This clustering increases with education. Conservatives, no matter who they are, cluster near the bottom.

The pattern we found in women's issues is seen here as well. Conservative employed women have the same *distribution* of responses as conservative men and housewives. Gender adds no information to the conservative distribution. In addition, education does not appear to affect the attitudinal patterns of conservative employed women. Just the opposite is true for liberal employed women. The higher their education, the more they are bunched toward the liberal end of these social issues.

Government Guaranteed Jobs

If we address more general questions of economic policy, perhaps liberalism will reassert itself as a more reliable map of the attitudinal terrain. Should the government guarantee a job and a good standard of living? This seems to be a fairly good measure of traditional liberal economic dogma. Is it an equally good predictor of individual attitudes? There are some interesting patterns here. Liberal employed women are clustered near the top, but about one-fourth of the liberal housewives and 20 percent of men are clustered *at the top:* Liberalism/conservatism appears to be more strongly connected to this issue for housewives than it is for employed women. The correlations between the two scales are .46 for housewives and .35 for employed women. Among employed women, however, liberalism becomes more constraining as education increases.

The pattern we noted above does not repeat itself here. Employed conservative women are *not* like other conservatives on this issue. On government guaranteed jobs, conservative employed women tilt more toward the liberal end of the issue than other conservatives. Some 23 percent of conservative employed women place themselves at the liberal points, while only 16 percent of men and 13 percent of housewives do so. This accounts for the lower correlation for employed women.

Although employed women are more sympathetic toward government intervention to assure people jobs and a decent standard of living (possibly because their own experiences with low pay and discrimination in the workplace have made them more sympathetic to the jobless and underemployed), it would be a mistake to overemphasize these differences. A substantial percentage of employed women feel it is not the business of government to guarantee employment. One thing is certain: If women are more compassionate, they do not reveal it in their domestic policy preferences—the connections are not overwhelming.

Getting Along with the Soviet Union

If women are not markedly more sympathetic to the plight of minorities, conventional wisdom holds that they might be more pacific in foreign policy. If men are macho and willing to face down the Russians, perhaps women, who bear the young who will die in war, seek compromise. However, conventional wisdom is wrong: there is very little difference between the attitudes of men and women in the aggregate on this issue. However, within women as a group there are interesting differences. Liberal housewives, those presumably with a more focused interest on youth, are (in a rare appearance) more likely to cluster at the top of the scale. They are more interested in getting on with the U.S.S.R. than either employed women or men. The differences are not stark, but are nevertheless suggestive. Since liberal housewives typically are not as liberal as liberal employed women, their attitude toward the Soviet Union bears consideration. Since few housewives have gone to college, an educational control is at best suggestive; nevertheless, liberal housewives with some college are more inclined to want to get along with the Russians than are less educated ones.

On the other hand, conservative housewives are more hostile to the U.S.S.R. than are conservative employed women. This hostility among conservative housewives *increases* with education, as does the desire of liberal housewives to cooperate with the U.S.S.R. The correlations between these two scales are .39 for housewives, only .20 for employed women, and only .22 for men. Given these kinds of interactions, it is not difficult to understand why there is no clear-cut women's position. Liberals, as one would expect, are more likely to favor cooperation, and liberal employed women and housewives somewhat more likely than liberal men to want to do so, but the differences are unimpressive. The most hawkish group in the sample are conservative men, followed closely by conservative housewives. The intragroup, rather than intergroup, differences are more important on this issue.

However, these attitudes changed in 1982 when Reagan's rhetoric challenged the "evil empire." Americans of all ideological persuasions became more cautious. Conservatives, one-fourth of whom wanted to increase defense spending in 1980, had abandoned this position by 1982. Only 4 percent wanted to increase defense spending. Liberals, only 7 percent of whom wanted to decrease defense spending in 1980, had increased their ranks to 26 percent. But this disillusionment with the military was shared by both men and women. Much the same can be said about arms control. Liberals disapproved, and conservatives approved, Reagan's arms control policy. Gender differences were minor. Even on the issue of the nuclear freeze, the gender gap is hardly compelling. Liberal women (48 percent) are more in favor of a unilateral freeze than are liberal men (34 percent), but the differences between the sexes are comparable to those within groups. Fifty percent of the liberal employed women want unilateral disarmament, compared to 36 percent of liberal housewives. These differences approximate the between gender differences, and thus do not lend support to the conclusion that women are more pacific than men.[5]

Nuclear Power

There are, however, two issues on which women emerge as consistently different from men: nuclear power plants and environ-

TABLE 3.8
Ideology and Building More Nuclear Power Plants

		Liberal	Moderate	Conservative	Liberal	Moderate	Conservative
		Total men			Total women		
Build more†	1	37.0*	47.9	63.3	15.1	20.6	33.0
Status quo	2	40.2	39.5	27.0	43.0	59.8	51.4
Shut down	3	22.8	12.6	9.7	41.9	19.6	15.6
	n	92	119	226	93	199	179
		Employed women			Housewives		
Build more	1	13.5	20.2	32.0	23.8	21.4	31.9
Status quo	2	38.5	54.8	46.4	52.4	57.1	61.7
Shut down	3	48.1	25.0	21.7	23.8	21.4	6.4
	n	52	104	97	21	42	47

*All entries are percentages. Columns may not sum to 100 because of rounding.
†1 = Favor building more plants.
 2 = Operating only those already built.
 3 = See all plants closed down.

mental regulation. The gulf between men and women on the nuclear power issue is remarkable. *Conservative* women are more antinuclear than *liberal* men (see Table 3.8). Employed women are substantially more antinuclear than housewives—who, in turn, are more antinuclear than men. Among both women and men the attitude toward nuclear plants is linked to liberalism: Liberals want to stop building them and shut existing ones down. Conservatives want either to keep the ones we have or build more.[6]

When education is added as a variable, the opposition to nuclear plants becomes even more intense—especially among women. Almost two-thirds of college-educated liberal women favor shutting down existing nuclear plants. Clearly, if economic problems do not finish off nuclear power in the United States, the heavy opposition of women will.

TABLE 3.9
Ideology and Environmental Regulations

		Liberal	Moderate	Conservative	Liberal	Moderate	Conservative
			Total men			Total women	
Unchanged†	1	63.6*	45.8	39.3	71.6	59.5	51.1
Relax little	2	11.4	6.8	8.9	5.7	11.3	6.3
Relax some	3	19.3	36.4	37.5	21.6	25.6	34.1
Relax lot	4	5.7	11.0	14.3	1.1	3.6	8.5
n		88	118	224	88	195	176
			Employed women			Housewives	
Unchanged†	1	75.5	57.4	58.2	47.4	69.2	52.4
Relax little	2	8.2	11.9	4.1	-	7.7	11.9
Relax some	3	16.3	26.7	30.6	47.4	20.5	31.0
Relax lot	4	-	4.0	7.1	5.3	2.6	4.8
n		49	101	98	19	39	42

*All entries are percentages. Columns may not sum to 100 because of rounding.
†1 = Keep regulations unchanged.
2 = Relax regulations a little.
3 = Relax regulations some.
4 = Relax regulations a lot.

Environmental Standards

A similar, if less striking, difference between men and women occurs on the broader matter of environmental standards, shown in Table 3.9. Here the normal pattern emerges once again. Liberal employed women are more adamant in their wish to maintain existing standards than liberal housewives, and, to a lesser degree, than liberal men. But liberalism is not as constraining for women as for men. For men, each decrease in liberalism yields a decline in the percentage of those who want to keep existing environmental standards. For women, there are less appreciable differences. Among employed women, majorities of all ideological persuasions want to maintain existing standards. Among housewives, the moderates and conservatives are more environmentalist than the liberals! Liberalism is a more reliable constraint upon the attitudes of men than of women. Among employed women, education increases proenvironmental sympathies among both liberals and conservatives (although not anywhere near the degree that it does on nuclear power). For women, there is not much of an interaction between liberalism and education on this issue.

CONCLUSION

Among women as a group, no clear evidence of a consistent and constraining ideology that knits together all the significant political issues examined in this chapter exists. However, within issues significant and consistent differences appear between men and women and between employed women and other groups.

On the four issues directly affecting women—the equal-role scale, the women's liberation feeling thermometer, the discrimination against women scale, and the abortion scale—the same pattern emerged. Conservatives, be they men or women, showed basically the same distribution across the issue scales. Conservative employed women are slightly more favorable but not markedly so. Liberals, on the other hand, differed significantly by gender. Liberal women were uniformly more favorable toward these issues than liberal men, and liberal employed women were more favorable than any other group. Liberal clearly means something different to women when feminist issues are involved.

Further evidence on this score is provided by the school prayer question and the two scales tapping attitudes about minorities—busing and government aid to minorities. These three issues fit roughly into the social issue category, although government aid to minorities has a strong link to traditional government intervention in the economy. The pattern is somewhat similar to the pattern on women's issues. Liberal employed women are the most liberal—they oppose school prayer, are the least opposed to busing, and favor government aid to minorities.

Clearly liberal employed women interpret liberal in its dual sense—economic liberalism as well as government intervention on social issues. This is certainly less true of liberal men. Although they are not Neanderthals, the gap between them and their conservative counterparts on the four issues affecting women is considerably narrower than the corresponding gaps between liberal and conservative employed women. The same holds for the three social issues not affecting women exclusively. The gap between liberal and conservative men is less than the gap between liberal and conservative employed women.

In sum, liberal women, to a much greater extent than liberal men, use "liberal" in its dual economic/social sense when issues directly affecting women are considered. Liberal employed women extend this dualistic meaning to some general social issues. That is, only liberal employed women exhibit *constraint* across all the issues. For men and housewives, it depends on the issue cluster.

To illustrate these differences further, we selected three women's issues (the equal-role scale, approval of ERA, and the belief that society discriminates against women), and three economic issues (the government should aid minorities, the government should see to it that everyone has a job and a good standard of living, and oil price controls) for comparison. Next, respondents who identified themselves as conservatives or liberals were divided into three groups: those who took conservative positions on all three issues, those who took liberal positions on all three issues, and those who took a mixed stand. This procedure yielded six groups: consistent conservatives, consistent liberals, inconsistent conservatives, inconsistent liberals, and liberals and conservatives with mixed positions.

The results are shown in Table 3.10. On economic issues, there are no significant differences between liberals and conservatives. On women's issues, there are remarkable differences in consistency.

TABLE 3.10
Ideological Consistency

	Liberals	Conservatives
	Women's issues	
Consistent	71.1*	12.7
Inconsistent	2.3	28.0
Mixed	26.6	59.3
n	173	379
	Economic issues	
Consistent	28.1	24.7
Inconsistent	4.4	4.5
Mixed	67.5	70.8
n	160	352

*All entries are percentages.

TABLE 3.11
Ideological Consistency by Gender

	Men	Employed women	Housewives
		Women's issues	
Consistent liberals	63*	84	71
Consistent conservatives	15	6	22
		Economic Issues	
Consistent liberals	26	39	28
Consistent conservatives	29	21	18

*All entries are percentages.

Fully 28 percent of conservatives took the liberal position on all three women's issues, while only 13 percent of the conservatives took the conservative position on all three. In contrast, 71 percent of liberals were consistent and only 2 percent were inconsistent.

If we break the data for the consistent groups down by gender category, we see that the women's issues produce a clear pattern of consistent liberalism, but economic issues do not (see Table 3.11). For example, 84 percent of liberal employed women are consistently liberal on women's issues. Only 39 percent are consistently liberal on economic issues. In contrast, among conservative employed women, *only 6 percent were consistently conservative on women's issues.* A remarkable 37 percent of conservative employed women were inconsistent on women's issues—that is, they took the liberal position on all three issues. Both conservative employed women and conservative men were inconsistent on women's issues. Some 27 percent of conservative men took liberal positions on the three women's issues; only 19 percent of housewives were inconsistent. This inconsistency of employed women and men produces the 28 percent figure in Table 3.11 for inconsistent conservatives on women's issues. Women's issues extract consistency only from liberals. Economic issues do not extract consistency from a majority of either liberals or conservatives. Nevertheless, Table 3.11 reinforces the fact that liberal employed women are *distinctive* not only from men but also from other liberals—housewives as well as men. *They view the world differently.*

NOTES

1. This terminology comes from Scammon and Wattenberg. See Richard M. Scammon and Ben J. Wattenberg, *The Real Majority* (New York: Capricorn, 1971), pp. 20-21.

2. The continued finding that tradition dies hard among those with the fewest opportunities to experience alternatives to their existing life-styles is one of the themes now being systematically analyzed by an emerging cadre of scholars, especially Sapiro. On the subject of isolation and incorrect information, she remarks: "We may assume that [the negative effect of marriage among the high school graduates] is due at least in part to the type of contact with feminism experienced by the women. At that time [the 1970's], the media tended to present feminists as a wild group of women who disliked men and liked to burn their underwear. No doubt the married woman whose only contact was via that image felt extremely threatened." See Virginia Sapiro, *The Political Integration of Women,* p. 78.

3. Fulenwider, *Feminism in American Politics,* p. 130.

4. See also M. Kent Jennings and Barbara G. Farah, "Ideology, Gender and Political Action: A Cross-National Survey," *British Journal of Political Science 10* (April 1980); 219-240.

5. For a contrary point of view see Sandra Baxter and Marjorie Lansing, *Women and Politics* (Ann Arbor: University of Michigan Press, 1980), chap. 4.

6. For comparable data, see Kathleen A. Frankovic, "Sex and Politics—New Alignments, Old Issues."

4
Political Participation

As the idea of women's liberation takes hold at all levels of society... it will become separated from the left-wing political milieu in which its ideas were first advanced. Women who are more or less conservative in other areas, including politics, will become increasingly assertive and willing to participate politically as this separation proceeds. This will be particularly true once large legal issues such as the ERA have been settled. Women—especially women who work outside the home—will be mobilized to participate at a level equal to that of men, but their mobilization will not be in a clear political direction.

Kristi Andersen, 1975[1]

Kristi Andersen's predictions, based on her analysis of 1952-1972 ICPSR survey data, have largely come true. We showed in Chapter 2 that the percentages of employed women and men who reported that they had voted in 1980 were almost identical. Overall census figures reinforce this finding. Table 4.1 shows the percentage of men and women reporting that they had registered/voted in the 1972-1982 elections. In 1972, 2.1 percent more men voted than women. In 1980, for the first time, more women than men voted. In 1982, men pulled back into the lead very slightly, but a remarkable turnaround has clearly occured.

Thomas Cavanagh, citing earlier voting studies,[2] concludes:

Gender was once a potent determinant of turnout, but its impact has all but vanished with the passage of time. In Chicago, Merriam and

Gosnell found that 75 percent of the men, but only 46 percent of the women, exercised the franchise in the 1920 presidential race, the first in which women were permitted to vote throughout the nation. The discrepancy between the sexes in Chicago was a less marked 69 percent versus 50 percent in the 1924 presidential contest. The same election attracted 73 percent of the men and 57 percent of the women to the polls in Delaware, Ohio. By the time of the early SRC studies, the gap between the sexes had narrowed to 10 percent.

In the 1964 census survey, the gap was about 5 percent; by 1972, it had fallen to 2 percent, and by 1980 it was 0 percent. In off-year elections, the gap steadily shrunk. In 1970, it was over 3 percent, in the Watergate election of 1974, it was under 3 percent. By 1978, it had dropped to about 1 percent, and in 1982, it was, for all intents and purposes, 0 percent.

Table 4.2 shows reported registration and voting by men and women broken down by age from the 1982 census survey. The .3 percent gap for 1982 is entirely due to older women (55 and over), who participate less than older men do. In the 25-54 age group, 49.7 percent of women reported that they had voted, as opposed to 48.3 percent of men. The clear import of Table 4.2 is that, in the future, it is highly likely that women will *consistently* participate more than men. Women in their forties and fifties vote more than men in the same age group. In 10 to 20 years, when they replace the oldest cohorts, the participation gap could become permanent and

TABLE 4.1
Registration and Voting by Men and Women

	1972	1974	1976	1978	1980	1982
	Percent Reporting They Registered					
Men	73.1	62.8	67.1	62.6	66.6	63.7
Women	71.6	61.7	66.4	62.5	67.1	64.4
	Percent Reporting They Voted					
Men	64.1	46.2	59.6	46.6	59.1	48.7
Women	62.0	43.4	58.8	45.3	59.4	48.4

Source: U. S. Bureau of the Census, *Current Population Reports,* Series 9-20, No. 370, and earlier reports. For 1982 data, news release of Monday, April 18, 1983.

TABLE 4.2
Registration and Voting by Age Group: 1982

	Men		Women	
AGE	Registered	Voted	Registered	Voted
18-20	35.0*	20.2	35.0	19.4
21-24	47.8	28.6	47.8	28.1
25-34	55.6	39.3	58.5	41.5
35-44	66.8	51.8	68.1	52.6
45-54	73.8	59.9	74.8	60.2
55-64	77.9	65.9	76.3	63.1
65-74	80.2	67.9	76.6	62.4
75+	76.3	60.2	66.8	47.1

*All entries are percentages.
Source: U. S. Bureau of the Census, news release, Monday, April 18, 1983.

favorable to women. At the very least, given the trends in Table 4.1, women will *not* participate *less* than men.

Registering and voting are only two forms of political participation. People participate in politics in many ways—bumper stickers on their cars, buttons on their lapels, attending political rallies, working in political campaigns, or just arguing with friends about the merits or demerits of particular politicians. Figure 4.1 shows a summary measure of six such activities (see Table 4.3) for men, employed women, and housewives over the past 30 years. The higher the number, the higher the level of political participation by the group.

Since 1952, the mean number of campaign participation acts for employed women, housewives, and men has fluctuated with the nature of the times. In most cases, the fluctuation for the three groups has been in the same direction. Note, for example, 1960, when there was an upward surge, and 1974, when there was a sharp drop. The trend is rather straightforward. Housewives do not participate to the same degree as employed women, but employed women are just about as active as men. Indeed, in 1972 and 1980, they were *more* active.

124 / Women, Public Opinion, and Politics

TABLE 4.3
Political Participation: 1980-1982

	1980			1982		
	Men	Employed women	Housewives	Men	Employed women	Housewives
Influence vote	.40*	.38	.27	.26	.18	.19
Attend meetings	.08	.09	.07	.10	.09	.05
Campaign work	.03	.04	.04	.06	.05	.04
Wear button	.07	.08	.04	.08	.09	.05
Belong club	.04	.05	- †	.04	.03	.02
$ to campaign	.11	.11	.08	.14	.07	.08
Total	.72^a	.75	.51	.69	.52	.43
n	615	390	215	633	367	221
n acts	442	294	109	434	192	94

*The numbers in this table are arrived at by dividing the relevant number of participation acts by the number of respondents.
†Less than .01.
^{a}Totals may not equal the sum of the columns due to rounding.

In general, the graphs for all three groups rise and decline together. Participation falls in midterm congressional elections, and rises during presidential years. The only exception to this pattern was an increase in participation by employed women from 1968 to 1970. The 1974 Watergate election excepted, the participation of men from election to election has been less erratic than that of employed women or housewives. Men tend to participate in off-year elections at the same rate as they participate in presidential elections. Employed women, on the other hand, increased their participation by .06 in 1970, decreased by .07 in 1978, and decreased by a large .20 in 1982.

This unusually large drop in participation by employed women in 1982 bears closer examination. Table 4.3 breaks down the participation index used in Figure 4.1 by category for 1980 and 1982. The sharp drop in the participation of employed women in 1982 is almost entirely due to the decline in the number that tried to influence how

FIGURE 4.1. Mean Number of Campaign Participation Acts for Men, Employed Women, and Housewives, 1952-1980

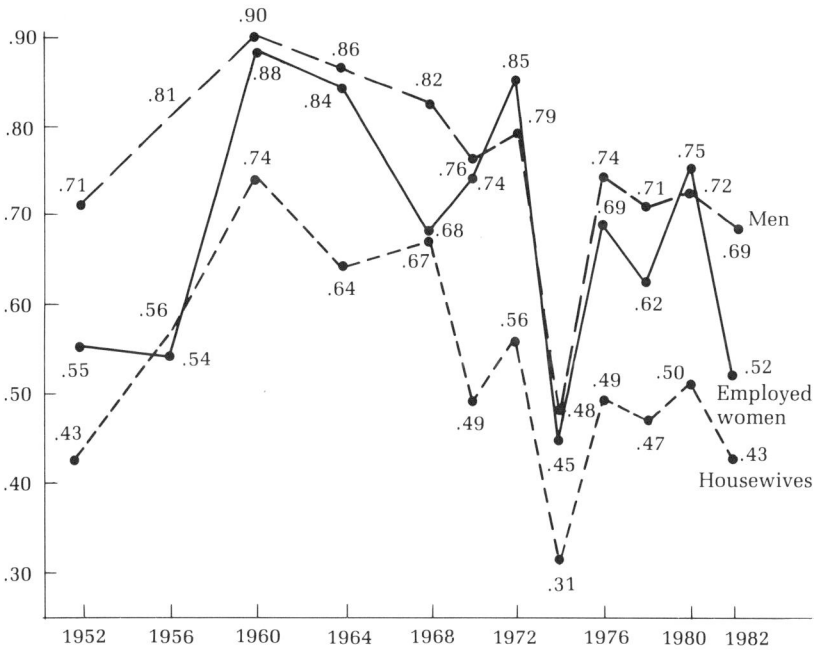

*1952-1972 data are from Figure 2, Andersen, 1975, p. 443.

other people were going to vote. Other categories remained relatively stable. Analyzing 1952, 1964, and 1972 data, Susan Welch found that "the one activity where men participate significantly more than women is an interesting one: whether the individual has tried to influence another person's vote. In this one particular case it does appear that women are indeed more politically passive than men, in that they are not as aggressive as men in trying to influence another person's vote."[3] Table 4.4 shows the influencing vote question for the past four presidential and off-year elections, respectively. The gap between employed women and men in presidential elections had largely disappeared by 1980. The off-year gap increased, however, in 1982. By this measure of participation, employed women were as apathetic as they were in 1974 and, for the first time, housewives were more intent upon influencing other people than were employed women.

TABLE 4.4
Influencing Another Person's Vote

	Men	Employed women	Housewives
		Presidential election years	
1968	39.9*	28.2	26.3
1972	36.8	33.2	23.4
1976	44.4	38.7	24.6
1980	40.0	37.9	27.0
		Off-year elections	
1970	30.8	27.4	20.8
1974	18.9	17.1	11.1
1978	25.7	21.5	14.9
1982	26.1	18.0	19.0

*Each entry is the percentage of respondents that said they tried to influence another person's vote.

The increase in the gap between men and employed women in overall participation in off-years, as opposed to presidential elections, shown in Figure 4.1, is largely due to employed women being less aggressive in trying to influence other people's votes. Other forms of participation are relatively stable from election to election. Given the duel roles of many employed women—as both wage earner and homemaker—it is more difficult for employed women to participate in politics. Consequently, they participate more in presidential election years, when the stakes are higher.

Housewives are quite another matter. Their participation has always lagged; in 1980 they were only modestly more active than they had been in the past, and in 1982, their rate of participation had fallen to its 1952 level. The failure of housewives to close the gap between themselves and employed women may well be attributed to education. Housewives are less educated than employed women. Since educated people participate more than the less educated, housewives are merely reflecting a universal characteristic of politics.[4] If we look at the participation rates of college-educated housewives, they do not vary much from those of college-educated employed women: In only three of the eight elections since 1968 has there been any significant difference. In 1972 and 1976, college-educated employed women outperformed college-educated housewives. In 1974, the reverse was true. Education, rather than occupation, seems to be the key.[5]

One very positive note in Table 4.1 and Figure 4.1 is the leveling off of political participation in presidential elections. The percentage of eligible voters participating declined steadily from 1960 until 1982, when it finally increased slightly. Figure 4.1 shows that this is true of other forms of participation as well.

PARTISANSHIP AND PARTICIPATION

Both women and men respond to elections according to their attraction to the nominee of their party. In 1968, Hubert Humphrey was nominated by the Democrats without having won a single primary. The convention was rocked with protest, and a flawed campaign began. By 1972, the process had been revolutionized by the introduction of a large number of additional presidential primaries, now the dominant mode of selecting presidential candidates. George McGovern carried the banner of reform with no success—arguably the most unrepresentative candidate of a major party in the nation's history. By 1976, post-Watergate, we entered the era of the media candidate: Candidates began their campaigns early, spent lots of money, and cultivated the media. Carter was able to nip old political pro Ford, but lost himself to a better media candidate.

The response to these elections is almost a chronicle of the times. Table 4.5 shows that, in 1968, male Democratic voters were the most active group; more active than their Republican counterparts, and more active than employed women who shared their preference for Humphrey. Housewives, in contrast, got behind Nixon. They worked harder for the more conservative candidate, a trend which holds with the notable exception of 1972. In that year the doomed McGovern enjoyed a substantial edge in participation among men and employed women, but not among housewives. Still, the pattern was set: Men and employed women outparticipate housewives. But in 1976, the partisan pattern reversed itself. Now the Republicans enjoyed the participatory advantage. All Republican voters were more active than their Democratic counterparts, and the gap was especially apparent among housewives. Republican housewives either hated Carter or loved Ford, since their rate of participation was almost twice that of Democratic housewives.

The 1980 election, which we discussed at length in Chapter 2, is important here for several reasons. First of all, *the most active group was Republican employed women* and they were working for a candidate stigmatized by feminist organizations! Ronald Reagan was the beneficiary of increased female participation, especially among employed women, but also among housewives. In fact, 1980 appeared as almost the reverse image of the earlier ideological election in 1972. In 1972, McGovern, the more liberal candidate, benefited from increased activity among employed women. In 1980 this advantage went to Reagan. Since we have described the results of 1980 as in large part a revulsion against Carter, rather than a preference for Reagan's ideology, these data should be interpreted with caution. However, there is room for speculation. In the years prior to 1976 (that is, before the massive influx of women into the labor force), employed women who were Democratic partisans were more active; after 1976, Republican employed women were more

TABLE 4.5
Mean Participation Acts

	1968*		1972*	
	Nixon	Humphrey	Nixon	McGovern
Men	.86	1.04	.83	1.23
Employed women	.76	.87	.80	1.42
Housewives	.84	.70	.76	.78
	1976		1980		
	Ford	Carter	Reagan	Carter	Anderson
Men	1.02	.94	.80	.69	1.14
Employed women	.97	.85	1.17	.80	.63
Housewives	.92	.52	.94	.71	.70

*1968 and 1972 data are from Table 4, Andersen, 1975, p. 450.

active. The same pattern, in less extreme form, appears for housewives.

For whatever reasons, Republicans gain from the increased activity of women. For 1972 to 1976 we used our awareness measure (see Chapter 1) to predict participation. One consistent pattern emerged: the largest contribution made by awareness to participation is among the college-educated employed women. They are the only group for which awareness is of any value as a predictor. Among the college-educated employed women, the rate of participation of aware women is between two and four times as great as for unaware ones. College-educated employed women are, in short, nobody's fools. Nor are they in any party's pocket. They are active, but not committed. Because their numbers will surely increase, both parties will want to court this group.

TRUST AND CYNICISM

It is now widely understood that the late 1960s and the 1970s were years of intense, bitter distrust of government. The cynicism of our commitment in Vietnam, the lies of Watergate, and the disruption of our cities was nearly enough to shatter the faith of even the most jingoistic nationalist. One explanation given for the across-the-board decline in participation is that people were "turned off" by government due to the shock of John F. Kennedy's assasination, Vietnam, the great urban riots, and, finally, Watergate. Figure 4.2 certainly lends support to this view. It shows the percentage of men, employed women, and housewives who gave no trusting answers or only one trusting answer to a battery of five questions designed by the ICPSR to tap people's cynicism/trust of government.[6]

Men, employed women, and housewives became dramatically more suspicious in the years from 1968 to 1980. In 1968, less than one-third of these groups were nontrusting. By 1980, a majority of each group gave, at most, one trusting answer. The step-level increase due to Watergate (1972-1974) is quite striking. Even after Watergate, however, mistrust of government continued to climb within all three groups—although at a reduced rate. Interestingly, the fall of the government from grace did not occur at the same rate

FIGURE 4.2. Trust in Government: 1968-1980

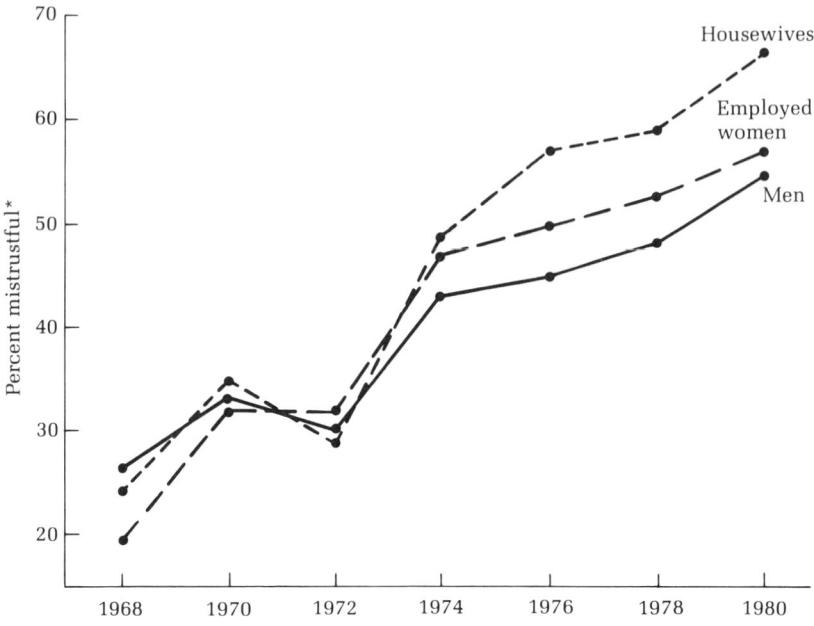

*Percent giving only 0 or one trusting answer.

within the groups. The rate of increase for housewives exceeds that of the other two groups.

The normal growth of lack of trust is revealed in the steady increase of employed women and men in Figure 4.2. The abnormal increase in suspicion on the part of housewives after 1974 requires some looking into. There are several explanations for the unusually strong growth in cynicism among housewives. One of the most popular explanations is that housewives, once liberated from the traditional attitudes which surround the role, will understand their oppression. This hypothesis does not work very well, however. In general, feminist attitudes are related to *trust,* not the *lack* of it. However, the relationship between trust and feminism does not hold true for housewives. Employed women with a high level of trust are more egalitarian than those who are less trusting, but this is not the case for housewives. They are both less trusting *and* less egalitarian than employed women. Another hypothesis is that education interacts with trust differently for housewives than for others. This

TABLE 4.6
Cynicism and Trust in Government by Education

	High school	Some college	College
1968			
Men	30*	18	18
Employed women	23	17	14
Housewives	25	27	7
1970			
Men	40	28	20
Employed women	34	30	28
Housewives	38	25	28
1972			
Men	37	31	23
Employed women	38	22	43
Housewives	32	26	24
1974			
Men	51	38	34
Employed women	55	41	38
Housewives	54	46	31
1976			
Men	52	42	31
Employed women	45	43	48
Housewives	62	53	42
1978			
Men	54	48	37
Employed women	56	51	47
Housewives	60	56	53
1980			
Men	56	57	53
Employed women	59	60	52
Housewives	67	62	72

*Each entry is the percentage of the indicated group that gave zero or only one trusting response to the five questions listed in Note 3 at the end of this chapter.

explanation makes a good deal of sense. Uneducated people have traditionally been less trusting than educated ones. Our data support this conclusion. Table 4.6 breaks down the data displayed in Figure 4.2 by our three gender categories. In 1974, for example, the nontrusting constituted a majority of men, employed women, and housewives. (1974 is a watershed year in the history of cynicism, it being the first year that a majority of nontrusting respondents appeared.) Cynicism remained relatively stable in all groups after 1974, with the exception of college-educated housewives, whose cynicism continued to grow. By 1980, majorities of all groups at all levels of education were cynical—an education no longer separated the cynical from the trusting. Since housewives were first as a cynical majority, it is fitting that among all educational groups, the 1980 housewives were the least trusting. Their lack of trust is pervasive: The college-educated housewives are *less* trusting than those with less education. Thus, since 1974, cynicism has increased more among housewives than among other segments of the population, and it has increased among the better educated.

Unfortunately, only three of the five cynicism/trust questions were asked in the 1982 ICPSR survey. A comparison of the responses to these three questions in 1980 and 1982 reveals that the leveling off in participation has been accompanied by increasing trust in government. Table 4.7 shows that there has been an across-the-board increase in trust. Without exception, a higher precentage of every group gave the trusting answer on each of the three questions in 1982.

Even though the percentages giving trusting answers increased somewhat in comparison with recent history, Table 4.7 is a sobering chronicle of the overall loss of faith in American government over 14 short years. Sixty percent trusted the government in Washington to do the right thing in 1968. Even with the increase in 1982, barely a third of the public was that trusting 14 years later. In 1968, over half the people felt that government was run for the benefit of all and not just for a few big interests. By 1980, only about 22 percent felt that way. The differences on this question between men, on the one hand, and employed women and housewives, on the other, are quite interesting. Over 10 percent more women than men felt that government was run for the benefit of all in 1968. Not until 1974 did employed women become less trusting than men. Housewives were more trusting until 1978.

TABLE 4.7
Cynicism/Trust Questions: 1968-1982

	Men	Employed women	Housewives
	Trust government to do right		
1968	61.5*	65.3	62.4
1970	54.4	50.4	56.4
1972	52.2	56.5	52.8
1974	39.2	33.5	33.6
1976	35.5	35.4	32.3
1978	34.3	30.9	26.5
1980	26.0	24.1	23.4
1982	35.4	33.1	31.2
	Government wastes money		
1968	34.6	45.3	48.4
1970	27.5	34.9	35.0
1972	26.4	35.4	30.9
1974	22.6	24.5	25.6
1976	22.7	24.2	23.2
1978	20.2	22.9	19.6
1980	18.3	21.4	20.0
1982	29.4	38.2	31.3
	Government run for all		
1968	51.3	64.9	62.3
1970	43.8	48.1	43.9
1972	44.7	49.3	51.1
1974	27.1	23.6	29.8
1976	26.3	23.4	32.4
1978	27.3	27.8	24.2
1980	21.9	23.6	22.0
1982	35.1	32.1	32.8

*Each entry is the percentage of indicated respondents giving the trusting response to the respective question.

The approximate 10 percent increase for all three groups in 1982 is very odd in light of Reagan's presidential style. Ronald and Nancy Reagan's enjoyment of the good life and association with wealthy friends was highlighted by the news media. However, this "rich man's president" image did not increase the number of people who felt their government was in the hands of the big interests—quite the contrary. Perhaps Reagan's budget cuts and loud howls by a myriad of affected interest groups convinced many that Ronald Reagan really was independent of the special interests and was fighting for the "people" (i.e., the middle class).

The government waste question in Table 4.7 shows similar patterns to the government run for all the people question. In 1968, substantially fewer men felt that government did not waste a lot of the taxpayers' money. This gap all but disappeared by 1976—roughly the same time as the disappearance of the gap on the government representativeness question. The increase in the percentage of people who though the government did not waste their money from 1980-1982—coming as it did after a steady decline since 1968—is eloquent testimony to the impact of Ronald Reagan on the public perception of government. The intriguing thing about the increase is that it is greatest for employed women—a 17 percent increase in two years. The fact that employed women are underpaid and are more likely to be hurt, directly or indirectly, by cuts in social programs (e.g., child care), probably accounts for this. The beneficiaries of these programs do not, by and large, regard them as government waste, and cuts in these programs will heighten feelings. Still, almost 62 percent of employed women in 1982 felt that the government wasted their money. Although employed women lean to the Democratic party, the old tax and spend philosophy of the 1960s does not have great mileage, even with this group.

The changes in attitude about government waste are consistent with the changes in support for defense and government spending that we discussed in Chapters 2 and 3. There was a significant shift of opinion across the board in 1982 against the core of Reagans' program of smaller government, but, paradoxically, larger defense. Evidently Reagan's budget cuts, and the pain that they caused, convinced many people that government may not waste as much money as they thought.

TRUST AND PARTICIPATION

There certainly is no denying that people became more cynical and mistrustful of their government during the 1960s and 1970s, and this affected the across-the-board decline in political participation during the same period. The causality, however, is not entirely clear. For example, as Figure 4.2 shows, about 60 percent of the respondents in 1980 gave at most one trustful answer to the five trust questions. Yet, as Table 4.1 shows, 59 percent of the census survey respondents reported that they had voted. Clearly a hefty percentage of the mistrustful people voted. Furthermore, between 1972 and 1980, the percentage of mistrustful citizens increased at a greater rate than the decline in voter turnout. The percentage of mistrustful respondents increased from about 30 percent in 1972 to about 50 percent in 1976, and about 60 percent in 1980. In contrast, the actual voter turnout in 1972, 1976, and 1980 was 55.7, 54.4, and 52.3 percent respectively—an overall 3.4 percentage point drop. *Reported* turnout (Table 4.1) declined from about 63 percent in 1972 to about 59 percent in 1980—approximately a 4 percent decline. In sum, the total mistrustful nearly doubled between 1972 and 1980, yet turnout dropped only about 4 percent.

All things being equal, one might expect that an increase in cynicism about politics and government would lead to voter apathy and a decline in turnout. However, the causality may go in the opposite direction. Mistrust can be accompanied by *anger* at politicians, and voters can go to the polls to punish incumbents. Given that turnout declined between 1960 and 1980, apparently the number of mistrustful/apathetic nonvoters was greater than the number of mistrustful/angry voters.

However, this may be changing—especially among women voters. Table 4.8 shows mean participation acts for men, employed women, and housewives broken down by trust. In general, the rate of participation of the mistrustful was about the same for all groups except for the 1980 presidential election. The choice between Jimmy Carter, who was perceived by many as weak and incompetent, and Ronald Reagan, who campaigned on a strong antigovernment platform, was enough to induce a sharp jump in the rate of participation of the mistrustful. They voted disproportionately for Ronald Reagan. The mistrustful voted two to one for Reagan;

TABLE 4.8
Trust and Political Participation

	Men		Employed women		Housewives	
	Not Trust	Trust	Not Trust	Trust	Not Trust	Trust
1968	.83	.83	.76	.67	.63	.71
1972	.67	.70	.71	.79	.42	.56
1976	.53	.69	.52	.65	.39	.49
1980	.66	.74	.78	.62	.53	.54

Carter garnered a bare majority of the trustful who voted. There were significant differences between the sexes. About 54 percent of mistrustful women voters went for Reagan, as opposed to 62 percent of mistrustful men. The figures for Carter were 35 and 31 respectively. Among trusting voters, women split 56 percent for Carter and 39 percent for Reagan; trusting men went 42 percent for Carter and 48 percent for Reagan. The depth of the disillusionment with Carter is illustrated by the fact that support for John Anderson was much stronger among the mistrustful.

EFFICACY

Political efficacy is the belief in one's ability to influence government. As Kristi Andersen points out: "According to the arguments advanced by the authors of *The American Voter* and others . . . a change in the level of political involvement should be accompanied by an increase in feelings of political efficacy. . . ."[7] Given that employed women and men now participate in politics at nearly the same rate, they should be quite similar in their feelings of political efficacy as well. This is indeed the case. Figure 4.3 shows efficacy scores developed by Andersen and charted for the 1952-1980 period for men, employed women, and housewives.[8] By her measure, women have yet to fully close the gap with men. Baxter and Lansing, analyzing the three efficacy questions included in Figure 4.3, plus a fourth not used by Andersen,[9] conclude:

FIGURE 4.3. Political Efficacy Scores for Men, Employed Women, and Housewives, 1952-1980

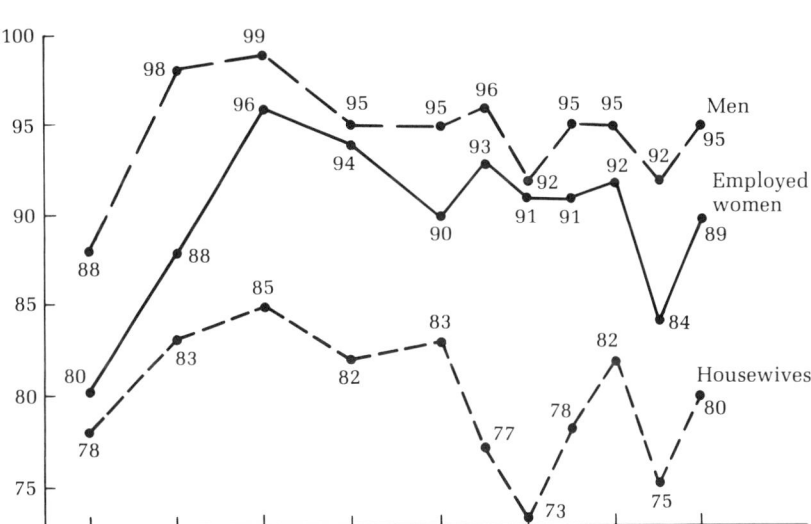

*1952-1972 data from Figure 3, Andersen, 1975, p. 443.

... women have an increased sense of self-esteem in political affairs today, but ... their level does not quite match that of men. Instead of interpreting the differences as an inadequacy in women, we suggest that, given the very limited number of issues that citizens can affect, the lower sense of political efficacy expressed by women may be a perceptive assessment of the political process. Men, on the other hand, express irrationally high rates of efficacy.[10]

Perhaps so. Unfortunately, the 1982 data cannot shed much additional light on this question, because only two of the efficacy questions were asked in the ICPSR survey. Table 4.9 shows the percentage of the respondents in our three gender categories disagreeing with the efficacy questions during the 1968-1982 period. What is striking about the responses in Table 4.9 is their stability. The responses within each group stay approximately within a 10 percentage point range over the 14-year period. Based on these two questions, employed women pulled even with men during 1968-1970, and have been equally or more efficacious than men since

TABLE 4.9
Political Efficacy Questions: 1968-1982

	Men	Employed women	Housewives
\multicolumn{4}{c}{*People like me don't have any say about what the government does*}			
1968	40.3*	41.0	44.1
1970	33.0	34.6	41.9
1972	38.1	35.6	46.6
1974	38.2	35.1	46.7
1976	41.7	35.4	44.8
1978	43.0	44.0	50.6
1980	38.0	38.1	43.0
1982	45.5	43.1	51.4
\multicolumn{4}{c}{*Public officials don't care what people like me think*}			
1968	43.4*	44.8	44.2
1970	51.4	41.3	54.9
1972	48.8	47.2	53.9
1974	52.7	47.9	54.2
1976	51.8	50.5	53.9
1978	52.6	49.0	56.9
1980	45.7	48.4	43.9
1982	50.2	43.0	53.7

*All entries are the percentage of respondents giving the efficacious response (that is, they disagree with the question).

then. Housewives, however, have shown no such tendencies. The gap between them and men has fluctuated, but has not consistently declined or increased.

Efficacy is clearly related to education. Well-educated people, whether men, employed women, or housewives, are more efficacious than those with less education. For example, Table 4.10 shows that 43 percent of high school educated men gave, at most, one

TABLE 4.10
Political Efficacy by Education: 1968-1980

1968	High school	Some college	College
Men	43*	17	10
Employed women	46	25	10
Housewives	44	22	11
1970			
Men	45	22	7
Employed women	43	21	4
Housewives	52	26	-
1972			
Men	46	21	9
Employed women	41	27	5
Housewives	53	30	14
1974			
Men	46	19	11
Employed women	48	14	14
Housewives	51	24	17
1976			
Men	55	25	8
Employed women	46	23	14
Housewives	54	28	6
1978			
Men	57	29	15
Employed women	51	35	13
Housewives	55	32	15
1980			
Men	43	22	15
Employed women	39	23	10
Housewives	41	16	33

*Each entry is the percentage of the indicated group that gave zero or only one efficacious response to the six questions listed in Notes 8, 9, and 11 at the end of this chapter.

efficacious response to a battery of six efficacy questions in 1980.[11] The corresponding figure for college-educated men was only 15 percent. College-educated employed women tended to be the most efficacious group. Although small sample sizes make the percentage scores for college-educated housewives unreliable, they have had the same pattern as men and employed women, with the exception of 1980.

Entering the workforce clearly reduces a woman's sense of powerlessness toward government. This is true throughout all education levels. If any group is guilty of "irrationally high rates of efficacy," it is employed women—especially those who are educated.

IF EVERYONE VOTED WOULD IT CHANGE ANYTHING?

So far we have seen that women now vote at the same rate as men and are likely to surpass them consistently in the future. However, although women now vote at the same rate as men, they still have not caught up with men on other measures of political participation. Women are not as aggressive in trying to influence other people's voting behavior. On the other hand, women—especially employed women—are somewhat more trustful of government and have a greater sense of political efficacy than men. Overall, men and women are becoming more and more alike in terms of political participation.

We know, however, from Chapters 1 and 2, that men and women differ significantly in their attitudes on issues and who they vote for—women tended to vote for Carter more than men did, for example. So, given that men and women participate in politics at the same rate and that they differ in their issue positions, what about the men and women who do *not* participate—are they the same as their participating counterparts, and, if they did participate, would it change anything?

Unfortunately, there are no simple answers to these questions. Nonvoters, on average, are drawn from lower income groups and are less educated than voters. Nonwhites vote less than whites and, until recently, women voted less than men. Because the Democratic party draws a large portion of its support from lower income groups, higher participation tends to help the Democrats. However, this

TABLE 4.11
Government Spending: 1980-1982 Voters and Nonvoters

		1980		1982		1980		1982	
		Voters	Nonvoters	Voters	Nonvoters	Voters	Nonvoters	Voters	Nonvoters
		Total men				Total women			
Reduce[†]	1	8.2*	9.5	13.7	11.1	8.1	7.4	8.6	9.1
	2,3	34.5	17.5	37.5	28.7	24.8	13.5	26.1	24.1
	4	17.4	17.5	25.6	28.2	21.6	21.5	29.4	33.2
	5,6	24.6	34.1	18.0	21.5	29.3	28.2	25.9	21.8
Don't reduce	7	15.4	21.4	5.2	10.5	16.2	29.4	10.0	11.8
	n	403	126	344	181	468	163	371	220
		Employed women				Housewives			
Reduce	1	6.8	6.8	6.9	6.0	9.0	11.9	13.7	15.0
	2,3	25.1	14.9	29.5	25.0	27.9	14.3	24.5	26.7
	4	21.1	25.7	27.7	33.6	22.5	14.3	33.3	31.7
	5,6	33.1	31.1	26.0	27.6	24.3	23.8	19.6	18.3
Don't reduce	7	13.9	21.6	9.8	7.8	16.2	35.7	8.8	8.3
	n	251	74	173	116	111	42	102	60

*All entries are percentages. Columns may not sum to 100 because of rounding.
[†] 1 = Government should provide many fewer services, reduce spending a lot.
7 = Government should continue to provide services; no reduction in spending.

does not necessarily mean that issue positions supported by Edward Kennedy and other liberal Democrats would be buttressed by increased turnout. For example, in 1980 nonvoters were more opposed to reductions in government spending than voters (see Table 4.11), but tended to think there was less discrimination against women than voters did. Nonvoters were more traditional on the equal-role scale. They thought the Bible was literally true more than the voters did, and they were more opposed to abortion. On the other hand, women nonvoters tended to be more dovish toward the Soviet Union, were more opposed to nuclear power plants than were women voters, and were more proenvironment. On economic and environmental issues, full participation would be favorable to the liberal wing of the Democratic party. On the social issues, full participation would be favorable to the conservative Republicans.

The issues of government spending and an equal role for women are instructive in this regard. We saw in Chapter 2 that the government spending issue most clearly separated Reagan and Carter voters. Table 4.11 shows that if everyone had voted in 1980 this issue would have clearly benefited Carter. Overall, almost 57 percent of nonvoters, as opposed to 43 percent of voters, placed themselves on the don't reduce side of the seven-point scale. The differences were sharpest among housewives. About 60 percent of nonvoting housewives were in opposition to a reduction in government spending. Forty-one percent of voting housewives were opposed—a 19 point gap. The gap between nonvoting and voting men was almost as dramatic—16 points, 56 percent versus 40 percent—while for employed women the gap was much smaller, only 6 points—53 percent versus 47 percent. By 1982, however, as we discussed in Chapter 2, the public had come around to Reagan's view on cutting government spending. The shifts away from the don't reduce government spending end of the scale are substantial for all groups, but are especially significant among nonvoters. The shifts were so large that the differences between voters and nonvoters were all but erased by 1982.

In contrast to their attitudes on government spending, housewives who do not vote are more conservative than their voting counterparts on the equal role for women scale (see Table 4.12). Approximately 47 percent of nonvoting housewives were egalitarian as opposed to 56 percent of those who voted. In 1982 the figures were approximately 41 and 51, respectively, so the gap between the two groups

TABLE 4.12
Equal Role for Women: 1980-1982 Voters and Nonvoters

		1980		1982		1980		1982	
		Voters	Nonvoters	Voters	Nonvoters	Voters	Nonvoters	Voters	Nonvoters
		Total men				Total women			
Equal role[†]	1	34.6*	35.6	36.6	38.6	36.6	31.6	41.6	40.5
	2,3	27.5	26.7	26.7	20.0	28.4	23.3	23.1	19.6
	4	14.6	16.4	18.7	22.9	18.0	20.5	17.5	15.5
	5,6	18.4	12.3	11.6	12.4	11.9	11.6	10.7	12.5
Place in home	7	5.0	8.9	6.3	6.2	5.1	13.0	7.0	11.8
	n	419	146	363	210	528	215	428	296
		Employed women				Housewives			
Equal role	1	41.5	34.7	46.0	48.3	26.5	26.7	33.3	22.5
	2,3	30.3	26.3	24.3	20.4	29.4	20.0	17.5	18.8
	4	15.2	20.0	15.8	17.7	16.9	18.3	20.8	17.5
	5,6	9.0	9.5	9.4	8.8	18.4	16.7	13.3	16.3
Place in home	7	4.0	9.5	4.5	4.8	8.8	18.3	15.0	25.0
	n	277	95	202	147	136	60	120	80

*All entries are percentages. Columns may not sum to 100 because of rounding.
[†] 1 = Equal role.
7 = Women's place in home.

was about the same. The differences between voting and nonvoting men and employed women were small by comparison in both election years. However, nonvoters tended to be more traditional than voters in all groups.

In our analysis of the 1980 and 1982 Equal Rights Amendment questions in Chapter 3, we noted that support for the ERA among women was most sincere. Table 4.13 throws more light on this subject. In 1980, 62 percent of women voters and 57 percent of men voters supported the ERA. In 1982, however, 59 percent of women voters and 51 percent of men voters were disappointed by the defeat of the ERA—a widening of the gap between voting men and women. The gap between the support of men and employed women voters is even larger. In 1980, 62 percent of employed women voters supported the ERA. In 1982, 62 percent were disappointed by its defeat. The difference in the level of support increased from 5 percent in 1980 to 12 percent in 1982—a seven point gap. The gap between nonvoting men and employed women was nearly the same. In 1980, 68 percent of nonvoting men and 62 percent of nonvoting employed women supported the ERA. Among nonvoters, men were the strongest supporters of the Equal Rights Amendment. In 1982, employed women were. The percentages were 56 and 58 respectively—an eight point gap between 1980 and 1982.

In sum, men and women were about equally supportive of the ERA in 1980. In 1982, women, especially employed women, were most keenly disappointed by its defeat. On this issue, full turnout would have helped the ERA in 1980. In 1982, full turnout would have made little difference—men and women canceled each other out.

Most of the issues in 1982 were like the ERA; although there were differences within the gender categories, full turnout would have made little difference. The distributions of all voters and all nonvoters were quite similar on most issues. There was, however, one glaring and significant exception: whether or not citizens approved Reagan's handling of the budget.[12]

The gender gap—especially between men and women voters—is clearly evident in Table 4.14. However, what is interesting is not the gap between genders but *within* genders. Nonvoting women actually supported Reagan on the budget more than did nonvoting men! If voters and nonvoters were combined, 47 percent of men and 42 percent of women supported Reagan for a five point gender gap.

TABLE 4.13
The Equal Rights Amendment: 1980-1982 Voters and Nonvoters

		1980		1982		1980		1982	
		Voters	Nonvoters	Voters	Nonvoters	Voters	Nonvoters	Voters	Nonvoters
		Total men				Total women			
Approve/†	1	29.6*	36.1	16.7	12.4	31.7	31.7	29.7	21.8
disappointed	2	27.6	31.6	34.3	43.8	29.8	32.8	29.0	31.3
	3	19.0	13.5	23.6	24.7	17.5	16.7	19.7	23.8
Disapprove/	4	23.8	18.8	25.5	19.1	21.0	18.9	21.5	23.1
pleased	n	399	133	216	89	486	180	279	147
		Employed women				Housewives			
Approve/	1	32.0	24.7	29.3	25.0	28.3	33.3	28.8	5.7
disappointed	2	30.5	37.6	32.9	32.5	26.5	33.3	23.3	28.6
	3	15.4	17.6	18.6	26.3	23.0	11.1	20.5	22.9
Disapprove/	4	22.2	20.0	19.3	16.3	22.1	22.2	27.4	42.9
pleased	n	266	85	140	80	113	45	73	35

*All entries are percentages. Columns may not sum to 100 because of rounding.
† for 1980: 1 = Strongly approve of ERA.
2 = Not strongly approve.
3 = Not strongly disapprove.
4 = Strongly disapprove.
† for 1982: 1 = Very disappointed the ERA didn't pass.
2 = Somewhat disappointed.
3 = Somewhat pleased.
4 = Very pleased.

TABLE 4.14
Reagan and the Budget: 1982

	Voters	Nonvoters	Voters	Nonvoters
	Total Men		Total Women	
Approve†	48.1*	44.6	38.6	47.2
Disapprove	51.9	55.4	61.4	52.8
n	362	195	378	235
	Employed women		Housewives	
Approve	38.4	47.5	41.4	53.1
Disapprove	61.6	52.5	58.5	46.9
n	177	120	106	64

*All entries are percentages. Columns may not sum to 100 because of rounding.
†Do you approve or disapprove of the way Ronald Reagan is handling the balancing of the national budget?

Among voters, 48 percent of men and only 39 percent of women supported Reagan—a nine point gender gap for those who participated. When men and women are combined, there is only a 3 percentage point gap between voters and nonvoters, so that full turnout would make little difference.

Although the pattern is not as sharp, it does appear to some extent on the other 1982 issue questions. Women *voters* tend to take the liberal position more than men voters,* but women *non*voters tend to take the conservative position more than men nonvoters *relative to their voting counterparts*. That is, the gap between women voters and nonvoters taking the conservative position on an issue is almost always greater than the gap between men voters and nonvoters taking the conservative position. For example, Table 4.15 shows the 1982 abortion question broken down by gender, voting, and nonvoting. About 43 percent of voting women opposed abortion while about 50 percent of nonvoting women were opposed. For men, the figures were 41 and 44, respectively.

The 1982 evidence suggests that increased participation would *reduce* but not eliminate the gender gap. Men nonvoters tend to be

*Abortion is a notable exception.

TABLE 4.15
Voting and Abortion: 1982

		Voters	Nonvoters	Voters	Nonvoters
		Total Men		Total women	
Restrictive†	1	9.9*	16.1	13.9	14.4
	2	30.6	28.0	28.9	35.3
	3	22.3	19.7	19.3	16.9
Permissive	4	37.2	36.2	38.1	33.4
	n	382	218	436	320
		Employed women		Housewives	
Restrictive	1	12.4	10.3	15.4	20.0
	2	23.9	34.6	35.0	41.1
	3	17.4	14.7	19.5	15.8
Permissive	4	46.3	40.4	30.1	23.2
	n	201	156	123	95

*All entries are percentages. Columns may not sum to 100 because of rounding.
†1 = By law, abortion should never be permitted.
2 = The law should permit abortion only in the case of rape, incest, or when the woman's life is in danger.
3 = The law should permit abortion for reasons *other than* rape, incest, or danger to the woman's life, but only after the need for the abortion has been clearly established.
4 = By law, a woman should always be able to obtain an abortion as a matter of personal choice.

somewhat more liberal than women nonvoters. The differences are not large but they are consistent. Full participation would not necessarily help advance the goals of equal rights activists.

CONCLUSION

Women's influence in politics will increase through the end of this century. Thirty years ago the voting participation gap between men and women was 10 percent or more. Twenty years ago it was 5 percent and 10 years ago, 2 percent. It is now 0 and very likely to shift in favor of women in the future. This, coupled with the ever-increasing percentage of women entering the workforce, is likely to shift American politics slowly leftward in terms of economic policy over the coming decades. This could change as women gain equality in income and numbers in the professions and other skilled occupations. Economic equality would likely result in women taking on the ideological coloration of their male counterparts. Economic equality, however, is not likely to occur in the near future. It could take a very long time.

In the interim, increasing numbers of women employed and participating politically will mean increasing support for redistributive economic policies. In other arenas, the effects are not so easy to predict. Men and women do not differ greatly on civil rights issues, for example. On some issues women are more conservative. Women are more opposed to abortion than men, and more opposed to busing, which they intensely dislike. On foreign policy issues women are more liberal. They are more in favor of a nuclear freeze and better relations with the Soviet Union. In fact, women who do not vote are more liberal on these two issues than their voting counterparts.

Predictions about the increased participation of women do not yield clear predictions about how the shape of the electorate might change—and we should hardly be surprised. Women voters, even the most educated and sophisticated ones, are not a bloc. Their votes are open to interparty competition. But what of women elites? Since the attitude of elites is generally more cohesive than that of masses, women office holders, for example, may be more consistently inclined to express a women's point of view. Of course, women still have minority representation in a male-dominated system. This may make them less powerful now, but it may make them more cohesive in the future.

NOTES

1. Kristi Andersen, "Working Women and Political Participation," *American Journal of Political Science 19* (August 1975): 439-454.

2. Thomas Cavanagh, "Changes in American Electoral Turnout, 1964-1976," paper delivered to the 1979 Annual Meeting of the Midwest Political Science Association, pp. 20-21.

3. Susan Welch, "Women as Political Animals? A Test of Some Explanations for Male-Female Political Participation Differences," *American Journal of Political Science 21* (November 1977): 721.

4. Sapiro finds that "privatization" (by which she means placement on the equal-role scale), motherhood, and homemaking are not as strongly related to participation as education is. See Virginia Sapiro, *The Political Integration of Women*, p. 122.

5. McDonagh finds, however, that homemakers married to men in relatively high status occupations participate less than their counterparts did 30 years ago. However, housewives married to lower status males participate more. Perhaps this curious result is a consequence of lower status families finding it desirable to have two wage earners. See Eileen McDonagh, "To Work or Not to Work: The Differential Impact of Achieved and Derived Status upon the Political Participation of Women," *American Journal of Political Science 26* (May 1982): 28-37.

6. These questions were: (1) Do you think that people in the government waste *a lot* of the money we pay in taxes, *waste some of it*, or *don't waste very much of it?* (2) How much of the time do you think you can trust the government in Washington to do what is right—*just about always, most of the time*, or *only some of the time?* (3) Would you say the government is pretty much run by a few big interests looking out for themselves or that it is run for the benefit of all the people? (4) Do you feel that almost all of the people running the government are smart people, or do you think that quite a few of them don't seem to know what they are doing? (5) Do you think that *quite a few* of the people running the government are crooked, *not very many* are, or do you think *hardly any* of them are crooked?

7. Andersen, "Working Women and Political Participation," p. 443. See also Sandra Baxter and Marjorie Lansing, *Women and Politics,* pp. 47-51, in which they extensively quote the earlier studies.

8. Andersen constructed the scale from three questions: (1) People like me have no say in what government does; (2) Voting is the only way people like me can have a say in what government does; (3) Sometimes government and politics seem too complicated to understand. The efficacy score was: 100 – percent agreeing with all three statements and + percent disagreeing with all three statements. Minimum possible score was 0; the maximum, 200.

9. I don't think public officials care much what people like me think.

10. Baxter and Lansing, *Women and Politics*, p. 51.
11. In additional to the four listed in notes 8 and 9 above, the questions were (1) Congressmen tend to lose touch with the people they represent; (2) the political parties are only interested in your vote, not your opinion.
12. Do you approve or disapprove of the way President Reagan is handling the balancing of the federal budget?

5
Women in the House of Representatives

INTRODUCTION

If women are to achieve true economic and social equality they must have an equal role in making and interpreting the laws that we all live by. More women must be mayors, legislators, executives, and judges. It is not enough that the law be neutral (if it is!); the interpreters (judges) and enforcers (executives) must be sensitive to women's concerns. The best way to ensure this is for large numbers of women to hold elective office. Only the physical presence of large numbers of women in the corridors of power will bring lasting and permanent change.

More and more women are being elected to public office, but the rate of increase, although encouraging, is not large enough for women to reach full equality with men anytime soon. Of the 7438 seats in the 50 state legislatures, 994, or over 13 percent, were held by women as of 1984.[1] This is more than double the 5 percent held by women in 1971. If this rate of increase continues, it will take women until the year 2000 before they hold half the seats in the state legislatures. The rate of growth in the number of women mayors of large cities (those over 30,000 in population), in percentage terms, looks spectacular, but such is always the case when something increases from almost nothing to a measurable value. In 1971 only 1 percent (seven out of 695) of big city mayors were women. By 1984, this had increased to 8.9 percent (76 of 854)—over an eight-fold increase. Most of this increase occurred between 1971 and 1977; about 2 percent of it occurred between 1977 and 1984. At that rate, it will be well into the twenty-first century before half the big cities are run by women.

In terms of long-run impact upon American politics, the growth of the percentage of women state legislators is more important than the increase in the number of women big city mayors. State legislatures are the primary recruiting grounds for future members of the U.S. House of Representatives and Senate. The number of women serving in Congress has more than doubled since 1969, when there were nine women in the House and Margaret Chase Smith was the only woman senator. In 1983, 21 women were members of the House and two women, Paula Hawkins and Nancy Kassenbaum, both Republicans, were members of the Senate.

Although the number of women serving in Congress has steadily increased since 1969, these numbers must be interpreted with some caution. In 1961 there were 19 women in Congress—17 women in the House, and Margaret Chase Smith and Maureen Neuberger in the Senate. From 1961, the number of women serving in Congress declined steadily, reaching a low of 10 in 1969 and 1970. It was not until 1975 that the number of women members returned to the 1959 level of 19. In contrast, the number of women serving in state legislatures slowly increased—from 341 in 1959, to 351 in 1963, to 362 in 1972.[2]

We are not likely to see a repeat of the 1961-1969 decline of women members of Congress. Much more likely is a slow but steady increase. This will occur not only because the major parties have concluded that women have to be taken seriously and have actively recruited women candidates for Congress in recent elections, but also because there are far more women in state legislatures, the legal profession, business, and management positions—the prime recruiting grounds. Of course, as we discussed in the previous chapter, the primary reason why the two political parties are taking women seriously is women are participating more in politics. A by-product of this is the increasing number of women running for and winning political office.

FIGURE 5.1. Ideological Makeup of the U.S. House of Representatives

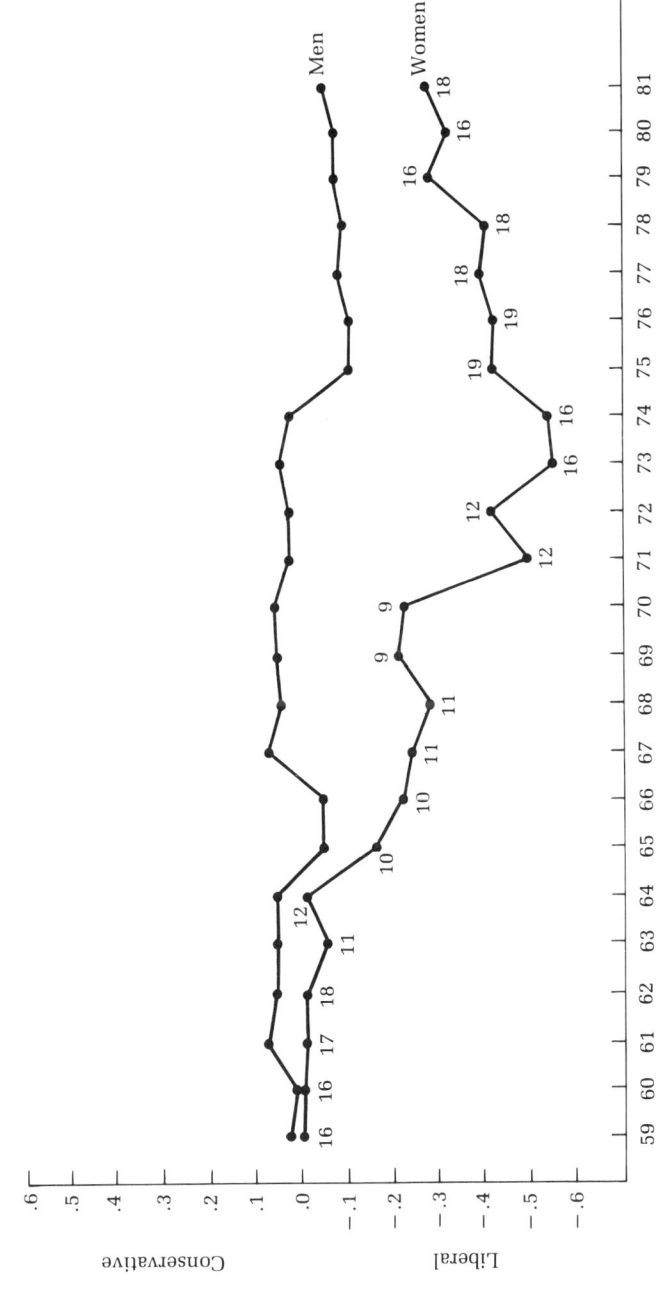

WOMEN MEMBERS ARE MORE LIBERAL THAN MEN

Women members of Congress tend to be more liberal than their male counterparts. Figure 5.1 shows average positions of men and women members of the House of Representatives on a liberal-conservative scale. This scale is constructed from special interest group ratings of members' voting records for the period from the end of the Eisenhower administration until the beginning of the Reagan administration (1959-1981).[3] Between 1959 and 1964, men and women were ideologically very similar. After 1964, however, they began to diverge. Women members are now consistently more liberal than men. The gap began to open in earnest during Lyndon Johnson's administration, which ushered in the Great Society and the buildup in Vietnam. The gap continued to widen during the Nixon years; women representatives became more and more liberal in their voting records, with the largest gap occurring during the Watergate years of 1973 and 1974.

Figure 5.2, which breaks down men and women representatives by party, shows that the large ideological gap between men and women in 1973-1974 and its partial closing after 1975 was due to the changing mix of Democratic and Republican women. Both groups of women are more liberal than their male counterparts, but the ideological gulf between Republican and Democratic women is about the same as the gulf between Republican and Democratic men. Between 1971 and 1974 there were three or less Republican women in the House.[4] Consequently, the average position of women shifted to the left. When more Republican women were elected after 1974, the mean shifted to the right.

Democratic men and women, on average, were significantly different ideologically throughout the 1959-1981 period. Republican women were virtual carbon copies of their male counterparts in the early 1960s. However, after 1966 Republican women in the House were more liberal than men, opening up a gap which became, by 1970, about as wide as that between Democratic men and women.

A partial explanation for the divergence of Republican women lies in the change in the type of women being elected. Women began to be elected on their own—not as replacements for their dead Representative-husbands. From 1961 through 1975 "41 different women served in Congress: 14 Republicans and 27 Democrats. A

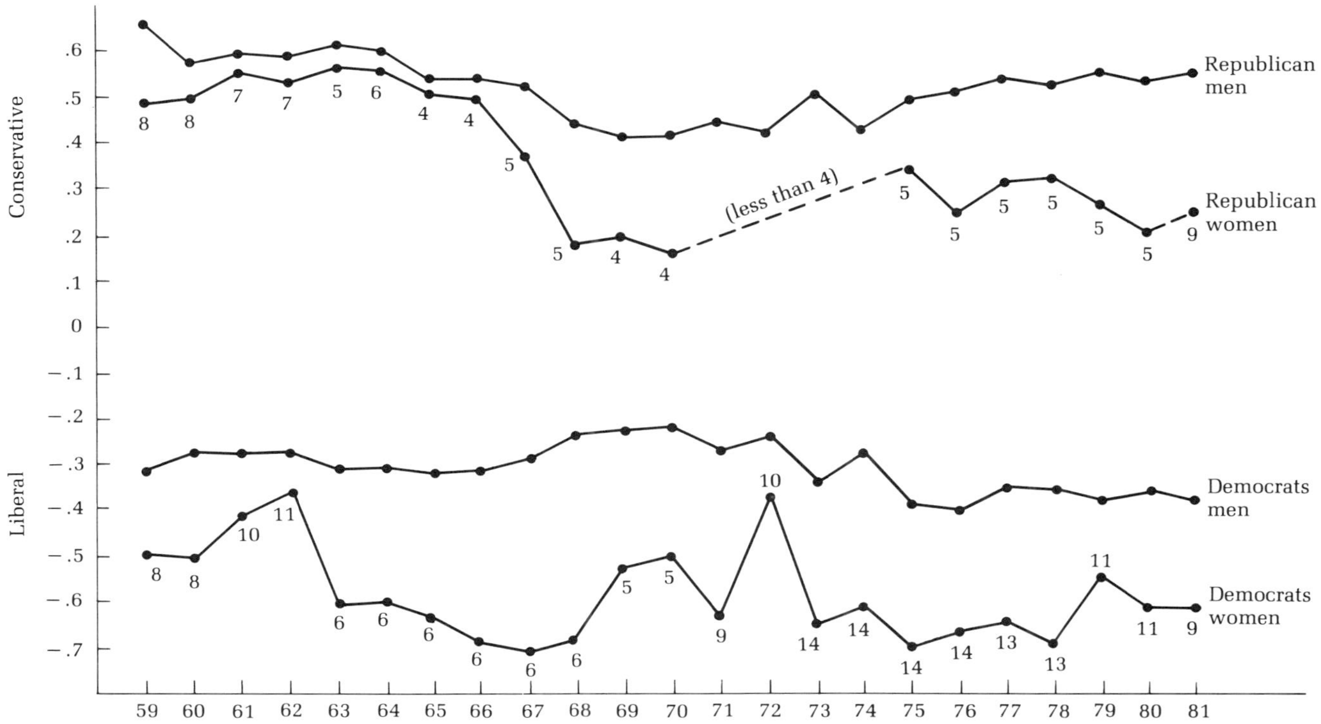

FIGURE 5.2. Ideological Makeup of the U.S. House of Representatives by Party

total of 15 had been elected on the coattails of their husbands: 6 Republicans and 9 Democrats. Of the 18 women in the House in 1962, 8 were widows; while in 1975, only 5 of the 19 women had husbands who had served in Congress."[5] Bullock and Hays found that, of the 77 women serving in the House and Senate between 1917 and 1970, 31—slightly in excess of 40 percent—were widows who filled vacancies created by the deaths of their husbands.[6] This state of affairs has changed radically in recent years. By 1983, only three (all Democrats) of the 23 women in Congress were widows elected to the seats of their late husbands.[7] We agree with Frankovic that "instead of the inexperienced, compromise-choice, Congressional widow, the average Congresswoman today may be more experienced, more independent, and more to the left of the average Congressman, and may have a less party-oriented voting record."[8]

The slow leftward drift of American politics that we forecast in the previous chapter is inextricably intertwined with the trends we see here. As the participation gap shifts in favor of women and as the percentage of women in the workforce increases, more and more women will be drawn into politics, just as they have been drawn into other professions traditionally denied them. Women members of Congress, almost without exception, have had at least some college education and most have college degrees, As we have seen in earlier chapters, such women are highly likely to be liberal and sympathetic to the women's movement and to be more sensitive to discrimination based on sex. Consequently, all things being equal, the more women there are in the House and Senate, the more liberal those institutions will become.

PARTY LOYALTY OF MEN AND WOMEN

Women Democrats and Republicans are more liberal than their male counterparts. However, this does not mean they are renegades within their parties. In fact, women members have tended to have party unity scores higher than new members.[9] (The score is the percentage of roll calls in which a member voted with a majority of his or her party members.) Table 5.1 addresses this point directly. It

TABLE 5.1
Internal Organization of the House of Representatives

Congress	Years	No. Roll Calls	Democrats Women % - Men %		Republicans Women % - Men %
91	1969-1970	21	+ 6*	(−10)†	5
92	1971-1972	28	11	(0)	−1
93	1973-1974	49	7	(2)	−5
94	1975-1976	42	12	(4)	−1
95	1977-1978	50	4	(1)	−6
96	1979-1980	81	1	(0)	2
97	1981-1982	38	− 1	(− 2)	−1

*Entries are differences between the percentage of pro-party voting by the indicated groups.
†Women % - northern Democratic men %. See note 10 in this chapter.

shows the percentage differences between the party unity scores of men and women where the unity scores are based only on those votes concerned with the internal organization of the House of Representatives. These votes include, for example, the election of the Speaker of the House, the setting of party ratios on committees, the authorization of committee investigations, the appropriation of monies for committee operations, and so on.[10] These votes typically pit the majority party against the minority party, and in many instances, they pit the northern Democrats against the conservative coalition of southern Democrats and Republicans. During the ninety-seventh Congress (1981-1982), for example, women supported their respective parties at almost the same rate as men. Men supported the party position at a level 1 percent higher than women in both parties. In general, Democratic women have supported their party more than male Democrats (although the gap between Democratic women and northern Democrats, shown in parentheses, is much lower), while Republican women have supported their party slightly less than male Republicans.

ISSUES THAT SEPARATE THE PARTIES

Welfare

Although women support their respective parties organizationally, they differ significantly from men in their levels of support for issues that lie at the cutting edge between the two parties. As Figure 5.2 suggests, women tend to take the liberal position within each party. Beginning with the administration of Franklin Roosevelt, the central issue dividing the two political parties has been the degree to which government should intervene in the economy. The Republican party has tended to oppose and the Democratic party to favor federal government regulation of free-market activity. This intervention has taken many forms: jobs programs, unemployment insurance, Social Security, pollution control, health and safety regulations, and so on. But the issue which really separated Democrats from Republicans in the 1930s was welfare, or *relief* as it was then known.

Most Americans today do not like welfare. The word conjures up negative images of lazy good-for-nothings living off those who have to work. However, when asked about specific programs—for example, nutrition programs for pregnant women and young children, hot meals for old people, help for the handicapped—people respond positively. The conflicts between the two parties are not over their existence; rather, the battles occur, for the most part, over levels of funding for the programs and over the rules governing eligibility.

It wasn't always so. Relief was the issue which began the great realignment of the political parties which political scientists now call the New Deal realignment.[11] It was government intervention in the economy in its most basic form—to keep people alive. Consider the situation in late 1931. Industrial production was only half its 1929 level. Farm income fell by one-half during the same period. Unemployment was nearly 24 percent. Those who were fortunate enough to still have jobs had to accept lower wages and fewer working hours. The impact of unemployment on families was particularly severe because far fewer women were in the workforce (only about one-half the present rate). The social programs that Americans under the age of 40 take for granted—Social Security, unemployment insurance, and welfare—did not exist. If you were without money, you either got food from charitable organizations or you starved.

President Hoover and the Republican party opposed any federal government relief programs. Hoover's position on relief led to the following famous exchange between George Huddleston (D-Ala.) and Carrol Beedy (R-Maine) on the floor of the House during the debate on the Reconstruction Finance Corporation in December 1931:

> [Huddleston:] With hundreds of millions the President would come to the rescue of the bondholders of the land banks, to the succor of the commercial banks, to the support of the railroads, and to the aid of industry of one kind and another. To these interests he would open the Treasury, but to starving men, women, and children he would not give a red cent. . . . The State is not in a situation to help. Uncle Sam can help, but the man at Uncle Sam's helm will not help. He hears our cry unmoved. Starving women and children appeal to him in vain . . . we have a man in charge of the Government who is more interested in pocketbooks of the rich than he is in the empty bellies of the poor.
>
> [Beedy:] Today I confess that I was amazed and somewhat disappointed to find that the majority party had given the floor in this first available hour . . . to a man who would commit his party to the principle that it is the legitimate function of government to go into the Public Treasury and take out money contributed to the support of Government by millions of our people and give it to a particular group which for the moment is in need. From that proposition, my friends, to which you gentlemen of the majority, judging by the enthusiasm of your applause, have acceded, we on this side of the House beg leave to dissent . . . men . . . have here acquiesced in one of the underlying principles of the Marxian philosophy.[12]

The intensity of this exchange still echoes in our politics today. It can be heard in the attacks on Ronald Reagan's cuts in domestic programs for the needy.

One of the most important modern-day relief programs is food stamps. Begun in the early 1960s with a budget of less than $100 million, food stamps were primarily a vehicle to dispose of the vast food surplus in the United States during those years. The program dispensed surplus lard, peanut butter, and wheat. It has since grown into a program with a budget over $10 billion and it feeds tens of millions of people per day. The food stamp program has been a battleground between the two parties for many years. The program is usually supported by a coalition of most Democrats and moderate Republicans and is sharply opposed by the Republican right wing.

Table 5.2 shows the differences between women and men by party and between parties on all food stamp bills voted on in the House during the ninety-first through the ninety-seventh Congresses. The votes included deal with eligibility requirements, authorization, and appropriations for the program. We computed the percentage of pro-food stamp votes for each group and the differences between these percentages are shown in the table.[13]

Before we turn to an analysis of this table, a few caveats are necessary. The differences in Table 5.2 and the tables which follow are comparable within each Congress because the percentage for each group refers to the same set of votes. Comparing these differences across Congresses must be done with a grain of salt, however, because different issue areas within a rubric may be involved.[14] In addition, control of the agenda may vary from Congress to Congress. For example, if all the bills coming to the

TABLE 5.2
Food Stamps

Congress	Years	No. of votes	Democrats women % - men %	Republicans women % - men %	Men D. % - R. %	Women D. % - R. %
91	1969-1970	3	19*	26	37	30
92	1971-1972	2	16	54	57	19
93	1973-1974	8	15	34	54	35
94	1975-1976	6	6	4	52	54
95	1977-1978	12	11	5	56	62
96	1979-1980	16	5	24	50	31
97	1981-1982	5	4	22	64	46

*All entries are differences between the percentages of pro-food stamp voting by the indicated groups.

floor for a vote are crafted so that they elicit the support of a coalition of liberals and moderates, then computing support percentages for our four categories will result in the scores for Democratic men and Democratic and Republican women looking very similar* and Republican men very dissimilar. Thus there would be a small difference between Democratic men and women and a large difference between Republican women and men. Conversely, if all the bills in an issue area during a Congress are written so they elicit the support of the conservative coalition, the difference between men and women Republicans is small and the difference between women and men Democrats is large. As a consequence, the differences are affected by the mix (in coalitional terms) of bills which may change from Congress to Congress. The larger the number of votes, the less important these two problems become. Even so, we will take the conservative course and focus on the directions (or signs) of the differences over time rather than the magnitudes of the differences.

One of the stereotypes that people hold about women is that, as Frieda Gehlen puts it, women are "supposed to be more moral, more humane, more oriented to the needs of individuals."[15] This stereotype suggests that women legislators will be more sympathetic to the poor and underprivileged. They in fact are. Women members of both parties in the House are more favorable to the food stamp program; this is especially true of Republican women. These results hold for voting on poverty and other welfare programs (e.g., AFDC) as well.

Jobs and Unemployment

Government activity to create jobs and reduce unemployment is intrinsic to the central issue of government intervention in the economy. Ever since the New Deal, Democrats have supported and Republicans have opposed efforts by the federal government to create jobs. From the National Recovery Act (NRA) and the Civilian Conservation Corps (CCC) of the 1930s to the Comprehensive Employment and Training Act (CETA) of the 1970s, Democrats and Republicans have fought doggedly over this issue. The divisive power of the issue is shown clearly in Table 5.3. What is

---

*Since most Republican women are moderate to moderate conservatives.

of interest here are not the differences between the men and women within each party—these are substantial but for the most part not too large—but the differences between women. Women Republicans and Democrats are somewhat more polarized than the men. Women Republicans may be to the left of their male counterparts, but they are hardly McGovernites. Women Democrats are on average 50 percent more supportive of jobs programs than Republican women.

General Interest Regulation

The original agenda of the New Deal Democrats, relief and jobs, has been greatly expanded by their successors. By the 1960s and 1970s, the federal government was seen by many Democrats (as well as many Republicans) as the instrument for solving many of the nation's social and economic problems. Regulatory agencies proliferated and the number of regulations issued began to grow geometrically.[16] Many regulatory agencies and regulatory programs were supported by Republicans as well as Democrats. However, some, like the much despised Occupational Safety and Health Administration (OSHA), were always bitterly opposed by the Republican party. The high water mark of conflict came during the Carter administration, when the consumer movement was unable to get Congress to pass a bill creating a Consumer Protection Agency. Carter had pledged to sign the act and had worked for its passage. It

TABLE 5.3
Jobs and Unemployment

Congress*	Years	No. of votes	Democrats women % - men %	Republicans women % - men %	Men D. % - R. %	Women D. % - R. %
92	1971-1972	14	10†	10	53	53
93	1973-1974	16	9	23	37	23
94	1975-1976	24	11	8	44	47
95	1977-1978	27	11	3	42	50
96	1979-1980	27	10	7	53	56
97	1981-1982	12	4	15	55	44

*No relevant votes in the ninety-first House.
†All entries are differences between the percentages of pro-jobs voting by the indicated groups.

TABLE 5.4
General Interest Regulation

Congress	Years	No. of votes	Democrats women % - men %	Republicans women % - men %	Men D. % - R. %	Women D. % - R. %
91	1969-1970	3	22*	14	26	34
92	1971-1972	18	15	32	39	22
93	1973-1974	57	12	13	31	30
94	1975-1976	79	11	9	43	45
95	1977-1978	39	6	10	32	28
96	1979-1980	55	0	16	49	33
97	1981-1982	15	5	12	34	27

*All entries are differences between the percentages of pro-regulatory voting by the indicated groups.

had passed both houses of Congress during the Ford administration but had been vetoed by Ford. The Democrats failed in their bid to override the veto. And, with majorities in both houses of Congress, Carter could not get the Consumer Protection Agency bill passed.

Table 5.4 shows the differences between women and men representatives by party on selected regulatory votes. The votes included in the table were general interest regulatory bills—that is, all bills with a potential for a *nationwide* impact: the Consumer Protection Agency, gasoline rationing, air and water pollution, the Federal Trade Commission, pesticide and herbicide regulation, and so on. In general, the votes we used involved "constraints on how funds can be spent, on the powers of regulatory agencies or the executive, and on private sector resource allocation."[17] The differences are those between *pro*-regulation percentages.

Again we see that Republican women are to the left of Republican men and tend to be closer to women Democrats than Republican men are to Democratic men. This is due largely to the fact that Republican women are far more supportive of legislation regulating air and water pollution. On this issue they simply reflect the differences between men and women in the mass public. As we saw in Chapter 3, women support environmental regulations more than men do, regardless of their self-identified liberalism.

Republican women are not consistently to the left of male Republicans on all regulatory issues, however. Table 5.5 shows voting concerning federal regulation of labor unions, long a subject of sharp controversy between the two parties. The votes included in the table were concerned mostly with the Davis-Bacon Act and the issue of common situs picketing. The Davis-Bacon Act requires that the "prevailing union wage" be paid workers on federally funded projects. Most construction involves a multitude of labor unions. Whether or not a single union should be able to close an entire construction site with its pickets is the common situs picketing issue.[18] Women Republicans are much closer to the men on this issue and are very anti-union in comparison to Democratic women. In fact, in five of the seven Congresses, the gap between the women Representatives was larger than the gap between the men. In two Congresses Republican women were to the *right* of their male party members. Women are to left of men on most issues most of the time, but not all of the time.

TABLE 5.5
Labor-Union Regulation

Congress	Years	No. of votes	Democrats women % - men %	Republicans women % - men %	Men D. % - R. %	Women D. % - R. %
91	1969-1970	2	34*	25	48	57
92	1971-1972	4	12	13	10	9
93	1973-1974	10	13	9	42	46
94	1975-1976	11	14	−3	54	71
95	1977-1978	22	13	3	58	68
96	1979-1980	3	7	−7	49	63
97	1981-1982	5	4	10	58	52

*All entries are differences between the percentages of pro-union voting by the indicated groups

Defense

Defense spending has been an important issue dividing the two political parties ever since the breakdown of the bipartisan consensus on foreign policy during the Vietnam war. Although there were controversies about defense programs and weapons systems in the late 1950s and early 1960s, these controversies did not equal the intensity of the debate that has occurred since then. Defense spending is now truly a partisan issue. There is some dissent within each party. The late Senator Henry Jackson, for example, was a classic New Deal liberal who believed in a strong defense. And it was, after all, John Kennedy who pointed to the "missile gap" and promised to defend liberty anywhere in the world. The Vietnam war changed all that. With notable exceptions like Jackson, Democratic liberals began opposing excessive increases in defense spending and new weapons systems such as the B1 bomber, the Trident submarine, and the M-X missile.

Table 5.6 shows that the women of both parties are in general more opposed to defense spending. Table 5.6 includes all defense department authorization and appropriation votes and all votes

TABLE 5.6

Defense Spending

Congress	Years	No. of votes	Democrats women % - men %	Republicans women % - men %	Men D. % - R. %	Women D. % - R. %
91	1969-1970	19	10*	10	23	23
92	1971-1972	37	11	28	27	10
93	1973-1974	63	20	16	27	31
94	1975-1976	68	23	8	22	47
95	1977-1978	69	13	12	28	29
96	1979-1980	59	5	9	24	20
97	1981-1982	71	7	17	28	18

All entries are differences between the percentages of *anti*-defense voting by the indicated groups.

concerned with national defense policy (arms control, troop levels in Europe, etc.). The gaps between Republican women and men are about the same as those on the economic and regulation issues (with the exception of food stamps). Democratic women, on the other hand, appear to be further to the left of Democratic men than they were on the economic and regulation issues.

The differences between men and women on military spending are consistent with the feminine stereotype of being more humane and pacific. The overall pattern of differences shown in Table 5.6 is remarkably consistent across the wide variety of defense issues included in the table. Table 5.7 shows only those votes directly concerned with the war in Vietnam.[19] The gaps are a bit larger. Women members were more opposed to the war in particular than they were opposed to defense spending in general.

Women of both parties have consistently been more supportive of the United Nations and other related international organizations. In addition, women members have consistently been more opposed to new weapons systems and have supported arms control more than their male party members. Stereotypes can be positive or negative. That women are more humane and pacific *when compared to men* could be interpreted to mean that women would be more balanced, wiser, and better able—if they were permitted—to handle tense international military and diplomatic situations. For example, if President Eisenhower had had advisors in 1955 and 1956 who were more humane and pacific, then perhaps better arguments would have

TABLE 5.7

The Vietnam War

Congress	Years	No. of votes	Democrats women % - men %	Republicans women % - men %	Men D. % - R. %	Women D. % - R. %
91	1969-1970	8	25*	12	30	43
92	1971-1972	13	21	37	42	26
93	1973-1974	18	19	17	31	33
94	1975-1976	16	29	15	33	47

*All entries are differences between the percentage of *anti*-war voting by the indicated groups.

been presented to him for *abiding* by the Geneva accords and acquiescing in elections throughout North and South Vietnam. The elections would have resulted in a victory for Ho Chi Minh and reunification. There would be no memorial wall in Washington D.C. engraved with nearly 59,000 names—almost all of them young men.

The fact that women members of the House of both parties support military spending less than men do is consistent with the differences on this issue that we discussed in Chapters 2 and 3 between women and men in the mass public. Women, regardless of self-identified liberalism, oppose defense spending more than men do. This was true in 1980 as well as 1982. We found in the earlier chapters that women did not want to reduce government spending as much as men did and that women were more in favor of government seeing to a job and a good standard of living for everyone than men were. These attitudes are consistent with women congressional representatives being more supportive of food stamps and jobs programs. In general, the differences between men and women in the House of Representatives are reflections of differences between women and men in the mass public.

There is one very interesting exception to this pattern, however—the issue of nuclear power. We found in Chapter 3 that the gulf between women and men on this issue in 1980 was remarkably large. Conservative women were more antinuclear than liberal men. Yet the differences between men and women members of the House are not very different from those for the classic liberal economic and defense issues. There were a total of 19 votes between 1979 and 1982 dealing with nuclear power. Women Democrats voted 9 percent more antinuclear than men Democrats and women Republicans voted 14 percent more antinuclear than Republican men. The difference between the two groups of men was 34 percent. The difference between the two groups of women was 28 percent. Women in the general public have a distinctive reaction to nuclear power. There is no distinctive reaction by women in the House; they appear to lag behind other women on this issue.

In Chapter 3 we found that two basic dimensions formed people's attitudes across a broad range of issues. These two dimensions were government intervention in the economy and government intervention to promote the civil rights of individuals and groups—the social issues dimension. The issues that we have analyzed thus far in this chapter tap the former dimension. The attitudinal differences we find here are consistent with those of Chapters 2 and 3; namely, women are more liberal than men within each political party but party is far more important attitudinally than gender is. We now turn to the social issues on which we found party lines to be blurred in the general public.

The Social Issues

Equal Rights for Women

Table 5.8 shows the differences between women and men for those Congresses during which voting occurred on equal rights for women. Included in the table are all the votes on the Equal Rights Amendment and the fight over its extension in 1978. Also included are votes on funding the Houston convention during International Women's Year. This table contrasts starkly with previous ones. When it comes to equal rights for women, women have no political party. Democratic and Republican women vote overwhelmingly for equal rights—the lowest percentage was 82 percent for Republican women in the ninety-fourth Congress. Nearly 50 percent of male Republicans and over 70 percent of male Democrats favored equal rights for women. The hard core opposition came from male southern Democratic conservatives and male Republican conservatives. All the support percentages are consistent with the con-

TABLE 5.8

Equal Rights for Women

Congress	Years	No. of votes	Democrats women % - men %	Republicans women % - men %	Men D. % - R. %	Women D. % - R. %
92	1971-1972	6	11*	29	38	0
94	1975-1976	8	19	34	23	8
95	1977-1978	8	22	44	30	8

*All entries are differences between the percentage of pro-equal voting by the indicated groups.

clusion we reached in Chapter 3 about the public at large. Men, regardless of political party, are inclined to agree less than women do that society discriminates against women. Male Democrats are more sensitive than male Republicans, but less sensitive than women Democrats.

Abortion

We pointed out in Chapter 3 that if ever there was an issue that cut across party lines and liberal/conservative economic lines, it is abortion. We found in Chapter 2 that abortion was of little use as a predictor of voting for Carter or Reagan in 1980. Men and women have almost identical opinions on the issue. Even when men and women are divided by self-identified liberalism the differences are not large. Liberal employed women, especially liberal employed women with higher education, are more in favor of abortion than other liberal groups. Otherwise the differences among the public are small.

Congress did not begin voting on the abortion issue until after the *Roe* vs. *Wade* decision in January 1973. Every year since then, it has been voted on in some form in both houses of Congress. The votes in Table 5.9 deal with cutting off federal funding of abortions, with prohibiting federally funded legal aid lawyers from helping poor women to obtain abortions, with restrictions on Planned Parenthood, and so on.

The attitudinal shift recorded in Table 5.9 is remarkable. Members of the ninety-third Congress were elected in November 1972, two months before the *Roe* vs. *Wade* decision. In this Congress, women Democrats were much more in favor of abortion than were male Democrats. The reverse was true of Republican women—they were more opposed than their male counterparts. In fact, Republican women (Heckler and Holt) cast no votes in favor of abortion at all. By the ninety-seventh Congress the situation had completely reversed. The nine Republican women in the House were now the *most* in favor of abortion, followed by Democratic men, Democratic women, and Republican men. The proabortion percentages were 64, 62, 53, and 20 percent, respectively. The only group to support abortion at a level of 50 percent or better for the entire period were Democratic women. However, their level of support has fallen steadily since the ninety-fifth Congress, when it stood at 79

TABLE 5.9
Abortion

Congress	Years	No. of votes	Democrats women % - men %	Republicans women % - men %	Men D. % - R. %	Women D. % - R. %
93	1973-1974	7	26*	−11	27	63
94	1975-1976	4	28	17	25	36
95	1977-1978	19	22	11	32	33
96	1979-1980	11	5	18	36	23
97	1981-1982	4	−9	44	42	−11

*All entries are differences between the percentage of proabortion voting by the indicated groups.

percent. This decline is puzzling since most women Democrats are highly educated liberals—the group we found to be highly supportive in the general population. Nevertheless, the conclusion we reached about the general public is applicable here. Party and economic liberalism are poor predictors of attitudes on abortion.

Other Social Issues

Table 5.10 summarizes the voting on other social issues that occurred in the ninety-sixth and ninety-seventh Congresses: busing, school prayer, and homosexuality.[20] Voting on these three issues resembles that on defense and the economic issues more than it does voting on equal rights and abortion. Women members of both parties are more in favor of busing, less favorable to school prayer, and more sympathetic to homosexuals than are men.

Voting on busing splits more along party lines than the other two issues. Republican women split almost evenly on busing, while Republican men were overwhelmingly opposed. In contrast, almost three-fourths of Democratic women and two-thirds of Democratic men supported busing. Although the general public is overwhelmingly opposed to busing, this is not reflected in House voting. The antibusing forces usually win by close margins but these victories are, for all practical purposes, meaningless. When the courts require busing to achieve integration it is usually the result of a successful

TABLE 5.10
Other Social Issues

Congress	Years	No. of votes	Democrats women % - men %	Republicans women % - men %	Men D. % - R. %	Women D. % - R. %
				Busing		
96-97	1979-1982	16	7*	28	44	23
				School Prayer		
96-97	1979-1982	6	5†	14	32	23
				Homosexuality		
96-97	1979-1982	3	34[a]	33	28	29

*Row entries are differences between the percentage of probusing voting by the indicated groups.
†Row entries are differences beween the percentage of anti-school prayer voting by the indicated groups.
[a]Row entries are differences between the percentage of pro-homosexuality voting by the indicated groups.

lawsuit brought by private individuals and groups such as the NAACP, not the Justice Department (which Congress can affect through strings on appropriations). Members who vote in favor of busing can justify their actions by defending themselves on the higher plane of constitutional law. For example, an attempt to deny the Supreme Court jurisdiction of busing cases (which Congress has the constitutional right to do) can be opposed on the ground that it is "dangerous meddling with our form of government" and has nothing to do with busing per se. Members of the House have been forced to vote on a constitutional amendment to outlaw busing only once in recent years, and it failed by one vote to get a *majority*. (Two-thirds are required to pass a constitutional amendment.) Since a constitutional amendment is the only way to rid the nation of busing, one has to conclude that representatives are not strongly antibusing.

Voting on school prayer is very similar to that on busing. On both issues, the Supreme Court is on one side, the general public is on the other, and Congress tries to avoid the issue. Large majorities of the public favor voluntary prayer in the public schools. As we saw in Chapter 3, large majorities of conservatives and moderates are in favor of school prayer, while liberals are split down the middle. (Gallup and Harris polls typically find that more than 70 percent of the general public favor school prayer.) We found that liberal women in 1980 were the most opposed to school prayer while conservative women were the most in favor. The only solid support for the separation of church and state were liberal, relatively well-educated employed women.

Voting in the House of Representatives is quite consistent with this division of public opinion. Large majorities favor school prayer. The least favorable group were the Democratic women. Their rate of support was 60 percent. Next most favorable were Democratic men at 65 percent. They were followed by Republican women at 83 percent and Republican men at a near unanimous 97 percent. It seems that school prayer is much like apple pie and the flag. Voting for school prayer in the House was undoubtedly helped by the knowledge that a school prayer constitutional amendment would be unlikely to pass in the Senate. This, of course, may change.

Homosexuals are not popular and if a simple resolution came to the floor of the House or Senate stating that homosexuality and homosexual life-styles are acceptable, it would not garner a large number of votes. The votes that did occur were concerned with restrictions on Legal Services lawyers taking legal action on behalf of homosexuals as a group.

Men and women voted quite differently on this issue. Democratic women supported homosexuals at a 77 percent rate. The second most supportive group were Republican women at 48 percent. Democratic and Republican men trailed with support percentages of 43 and 25, respectively. The more sympathetic view of homosexuality by women—irrespective of party—may provide some evidence for the popularly held view that men have a greater fear of and feel more threatened by homosexuality than do women given the traditional emphasis in our society upon "manliness."

CONCLUSION

Gender and party voting on the issues in the House of Representatives is basically consistent with attitudinal differences within the general public. Women are more liberal than men on the economic issues connected with the central issue of government intervention in the economy. Women representatives of both political parties are more liberal than their male counterparts in House voting on these issues. Women of both parties in the House support equal rights for women more than male representatives, which also reflects the division in the general public. The crosscurrents of opinion on abortion show up in the voting of representatives. Republican women support abortion more than any other group. On other social issues the picture is somewhat complicated, but the basic conclusion holds: Voting by women and men in the House of Representatives is largely consistent with the attitudes of women and men generally.

This conclusion should not surprise us. The framers of the constitution intended the House of Representatives to be the institution of government that would be closest to the people. They succeeded.

Although our main purpose in this chapter is to spotlight the gender differences of elected officials within the two political parties, it is important to remember that on core issues, such as jobs programs, the differences *between* the two parties are far more significant politically. They form the backdrop against which our discussion of gender differences takes place. The ideological gulf between women Democrats and women Republicans is as wide as that between the men. This is shown in Figure 5.2 and Tables 5.2 through 5.7. Women as a group are as different from each other in party terms as men.

We predicted at the end of Chapter 4 that American politics would shift slowly leftward because women are participating in politics more and an increasing percentage of women are being drawn into the workforce. In this chapter, we predicted that the number of women in Congress would continue to increase both because of the great rise in the number of women in the state legislatures and the general forces cited above. We are confident in our predictions. Public attitudes about women in public office are changing rapidly. A November 1983 *New York Times* poll found that 48 percent of the general public felt that Congress would be improved by having more women as members. Only 10 percent felt more women would make Congress worse. The rest had either no opinion or felt it would make no difference.[21] Furthermore, "a total of 69 percent of the women polled and 64 percent of the men felt that women were more sensitive to the problems of the poor and the underprivileged." In other words, the general public thinks women members of Congress would be more liberal than men members. The public perception is correct. In addition, the poll found that:

> While there are no polling benchmarks against which the 48 percent favoring more women in Congress can be measured, the finding still appeared significant. The earnestness of the volunteered explanations as to why Congress would be better with more women suggested that the answer was more than an off-the-cuff endorsement of equality.

The public is receptive and the number of politically experienced potential candidates is increasing. Women need no longer become widows to be elected to Congress.[22] The stage is thus set for a slow shift to the left on economic issues in Congress as more women replace men in each political party.

NOTES

1. The sources for these figures, as well as those for mayors, are the *National Directory of Women Elected Officials 1982*, published by the National Women's Political Caucus; and Judith Cummings, "Women in State Legislatures Speak Out," *New York Times*, 5 December 1983.

2. The 1959 and 1963 data are from Emmy E. Werner, "Women in Congress: 1917-1964," *Western Political Quarterly 29* (1966): 28, table 12.

3. For details of the scale construction, see Keith T. Poole, "Dimensions of Interest Group Evaluation of the U.S. Senate 1969-1978," *American Journal of Political Science 25* (February 1981): 41-57. The scaling methodology is known as *metric unfolding*. See Keith T. Poole, "Least Squares Metric, Unidimensional Unfolding," *Psychometrika 49* (1984). The interest groups included in the scaling included the American Civil Liberties Union, the American Conservative Union, the Americans for Constitutional Action, the

Americans for Democratic Action, the Child Welfare League of America, the United Auto Workers, the National Women's Political Caucus, and 35 other groups. These included fundamentalists (Christian Voice), farmers (National Farmer's Union, American Farmer Bureau Federation, National Farmer's Organization), organized labor (COPE, American Federation of Teachers), Ralph Nadar (Congress Watch), etc. Virtually every interest group issuing ratings between 1959-1980 was included.

4. In 1971, Charlotte Reid, Florence Dwyer, and Margaret Heckler served in the House. In 1972, Dwyer and Heckler were the only Republican women, and in 1973 and 1974 only Heckler and Marjorie Holt served.

5. Kathleen A. Frankovic, "Sex and Voting in the U.S. House of Representatives," *American Politics Quarterly 5* (1977): 318.

6. Charles S. Bullock III and Patricia Lee Findley Hays, "Recruitment of Women for Congress: A Research Note," *Western Political Quarterly 25* (1972): 416-423.

7. They were Corinne Boggs, Beverly Byron, and Cardis Collins.

8. Frankovic, "Sex and Voting in the U.S. House of Representatives," p. 317.

9. See Frankovic, "Sex and Voting in the U.S. House of Representatives," and Freida L. Gehlen, "Women Members of Congress: A Distinctive Role," In Marianne Githens and Jewel L. Prestage, Eds., *A Portrait of Marginality* (New York: Longman, 1977).

10. The group party unity score is the ratio of the number of votes cast with the majority of the group by the group members divided by the total number of votes by the group. For example, if the group had 100 members and there were five votes, and if everyone voted, there would be 500 total votes cast. If the vote divisions on the five votes were 70-30, 65-35, 80-20, 85-15, and 90-10, for example, the total party unity votes would be 390 (70 + 65 + 80 + 85 + 90). The party score for the group would then be (390/500) × 100 = 78 percent. The percentage support scores used to compute the differences shown in the remaining tables of the chapter were computed in a similar way. All votes with at least 30 votes in the minority were included. This criteria was applied to all the votes used in the tables that follow. Of course, party line votes, by definition, will have greater than 30 votes in the minority. There are votes, however, that pit all of one party plus part of the other party against the remainder of the second. This was true, for example, of many votes dealing with the House Judiciary Committee's investigation of Watergate in 1973-1974. They pitted the Democrats and moderate Republicans against the conservative Republicans (who were a majority of the Republican party).

176 / Women, Public Opinion, and Politics

11. See James L. Sundquist, *Dynamics of the Party System* (Washington, D.C.: Brookings Institution, 1973), chapter 10. As Sundquist shows, the 1932 election was not centered on the issue of relief specifically. Rather, what Roosevelt offered was *change*. In fact, Roosevelt's platform was quite conservative (he offered a balanced budget, for example). However, what really began to differentiate the *elected officials* of the two parties in 1930 was their stand on relief. This *philosophical difference* was and is at the heart of the difference between the Democratic and Republican parties.

12. *Congressional Record,* 72 Cong. I Session (December 9, 1931), pp. 240-243. Quoted in Sundquist, *Dynamics of the Party System,* p. 188.

13. The support percentages were computed as described in note 10 above. For example, suppose there are 10 women voting and there are five votes in the issue area. If the vote divisions on the five votes were 8-2, 9-1, 10-0, 7-3, and 6-4, for example, the total support would be 40 (8 + 9 + 10 + 7 + 6). The support score for the group would then be (40/50) × 100 = 80 percent. Note that this assumes that the majority were *pro* or in support of the policy on each vote (e.g., pro food stamp).

14. For example, we consider below the area of general interest regulation—gasoline rationing, auto pollution, and so on. During one Congress most of the voting in the general interest regulation issue category may concern gasoline rationing. During another Congress it may concern the Federal Trade Commission, and so on.

15. Frieda L. Gehlen, "Women Members of Congress: A Distinctive Role," p. 305.

16. "Perhaps the most striking commentary on the increasing regulatory role of the Federal government is provided by a perusal of the *Federal Register.* This publication of the General Services Administration contains updates of the various rules, regulations, and legal notices emanating from the executive branch of the government." Morris P. Fiorina, *Congress: Keystone of the Washington Establishment* (New Haven, Conn.: Yale University Press, 1977), p. 93. In 1956 there were 10,528 pages in the *Federal Register.* By 1966 this increased to 16,850. It increased to 60,221 in 1975, to 77,498 in 1977, and peaked at 85,650 in 1980. Under Reagan the numbers dropped to 63,553 in 1981 and 58,493 in 1982.

17. Sam Peltzman, "Constituent Interest and Congressional Voting," mimeograph, University of Chicago.

18. Some of the votes in Table 5.5 are also used in Table 5.4. The votes in Table 5.5 include many judged not to have a nationwide impact—the criteria used for selecting votes for Table 5.4.

19. These include votes on authorization and appropriations for the war effort, resolutions to cut off support to South Vietnam, and so on. Each vote was coded either pro- or anti-Vietnam war. The percentages in the table are differences between the respective antipercentages.

20. Votes on busing typically take the form of amendments to appropriations bills for the Justice Department and the Department of Health and Human Services denying authority to the departments to spend money in any way that promotes busing. Voting on school prayer involves similar amendments restricting the Justice Department from opposing school prayer. In the ninety-seventh Congress, a constitutional amendment permitting school prayer was voted on. Votes on homosexuality are concerned with preventing Legal Services lawyers from taking legal action on behalf of homosexuals.

21. "Poll Shows Support For Political Gains by Women," *New York Times,* 27 November 1983, p. 1.

22. See Diana Kincaid, "Over This Dead Body: A Positive Perspective on Widows in the U.S. Congress," *Western Political Quarterly 31* (March 1978): 96-104.

Appendix A

The respondents' perceptions of where the candidates and groups stood on the seven point equal-role scale in 1972 were used to divide the panel into two groups: those who were minimally aware of feminism and those who were not. This was done by scaling the data using the method developed by Aldrich and McKelvey.[1] This method assumes that the candidates/groups (or more generally stimuli):

> ... occupy true positions on an issue continuum, and ... the information that the citizen gives ... on his perceptions of the candidates is derived from this true position in a two step process. In the first stage, we assume that there is a random disturbance in the citizen's perception of the candidate.... The second stage consists of the voter taking what is in his head, i.e., his perceptions, and reporting them to the interviewer. Here, we assume, since there is no common metric for placing the candidates on a scale, that the positions where the citizen reports that he sees the candidates may be an arbitrary linear transformation of his perception of the space. (p. 113)

The least squares estimate of the true positions of the stimuli is essentially a principal components solution and the respondent

[1] John Aldrich and Richard D. McKelvey, "A Method of Scaling with Applications to the 1968 and 1972 Presidential Elections," *American Political Science Review 71* (February 1977): 111-130.

parameters—a weight and an intercept term—are estimated by regression. The respondent's scaled position on the underlying continuum is found by applying the linear transformation to the respondent's reported position.

A major drawback of the method is that no constraint is placed upon the respondents' estimated weights—they can be either positive or negative. A negative weight means, in effect, that the respondent perceives the stimuli in a mirror image space. An example of a negative weight respondent in 1972 would be a person who placed herself or himself at 1 (the equal role or egalitarian end), Wallace at 2, Nixon and the Republican party at 4, the Democratic party at 5, and McGovern at 7 (the place is in the home or traditional end). If this ordering of stimuli were exactly reversed, then it would be consistent with the configuration recovered on the underlying issue continuum (see Table A.2). This reversal or mirroring is precisely what a negative weight achieves. Therefore, when the respondent's linear transformation is applied to her/his reported position, it has the effect of mapping her/him onto the conservative side of the underlying issue continuum. This "backwards seeing" respondent then contributes to a better fit to the true space.

For purposes of this analysis, only those respondents with positive weights in 1972 will be included in the aware portion of the panel. This has the effect of excluding four groups: those who cannot locate themselves on the scale; those who cannot locate all the stimuli on the scale; those who locate all the stimuli in the same place on the scale; and those who see the stimuli in mirror image.

TABLE A.1
The 1972-1974-1976 Panel Study

	Number of Respondents
Total panel	1320
Locate self	1269
Missing data	625
Stimuli at same point	126
Scalable data	518
Positive weights	429

TABLE A.2
Scaled Stimuli Locations for 1972

	Nixon	McGovern	Wallace	Dem.	Rep.	I[a]	σ^{2}[b]
Position	−.033[c]	−.455	.831	−.316	−.027	−.322	.382
Std. Dev.	.384	.440	.566	.367	.372	1.467	

[a]Stimuli positions are constrained to have a mean of one and a sum of squares equal to one.
[b]Mean position of respondents.
[c]Estimated average squared deviations of the observed from the true candidate positions.

Clearly, respondents who perceive the scale backwards or who are unable to place themselves or one or more of the stimuli—Nixon, Wallace, and the two major parties—on the scale are less aware of women's rights issues than a person who can locate herself/himself and order the stimuli coherently across the scale. The respondents who located all the stimuli in the same place have to be excluded from the aware portion because there is no variance in their perceptions, and weights cannot be estimated for them. This filtering divides the total panel of 1,320 into 429 aware and 891 unaware respondents. Because we are primarily interested in individual change over time, missing data in 1974 and/or 1976 reduce the actual number of aware and unaware respondents to between 285 and 305 and between 670 and 750 respectively, depending upon the items we are using. Table A.1 breaks down the panel data along these lines, and Table A.2 displays the 1972 scaled locations of the stimuli.

Unfortunately, we cannot perform a similar analysis on the seven point scale data in 1976—which would allow us to directly measure the change in awareness over the period—because the response task in 1976 was quite different. The only stimuli in common in the two years were the two major political parties. Accordingly, we will be forced to measure the change in awareness indirectly. For example, by comparing the rates of change of support for feminism as well as the rates of change in constraint for the unaware and aware groups, we will be able to infer changes in awareness as well.

Appendix B

Table B.1 elaborates upon Figure 1.1. The table is divided into two parts. The left half of the table shows the results for the five cross-sectional surveys taken during the period, while the right half shows the results for the 1972-1974-1976 panel study. In the table we have collapsed scale positions 2, 3 (moderate egalitarianism) and 5, 6 (moderate traditionalism), while allowing the extreme positions to remain as recorded. A more traditional method (collapsing the first two and last two positions) would have lost an essential aspect of the response to the question; namely, the attitudinal movement of the panel of respondents reveals a loss of enthusiasm for both the extreme egalitarian and extreme traditional points of view.

Table B.2 elaborates upon Table 1.1. It shows how men, employed women, and housewives were distributed by education across the equal-role scale from 1972 to 1982.

Table B.3 is the detailed counterpart to Table 1.8. It shows the distribution by awareness of men, employed women, and housewives across the equal-role scale. Table B.4 shows the mean women's liberation feeling thermometer scores by the three gender categories. Table B.5 is our final table dealing with awareness. It shows the percentage of pro- and antifeminist responses to five attitude questions asked in 1972 and 1976. The responses are crosstabbed by the two years and are broken down by awareness and gender. For example, 37.1 percent of the responses of aware housewives in the 1972-1976 panel were profeminist in both years. Note that we are

TABLE B.1
Attitudes of Men, Employed Women, and Housewives on an Equal Role for Women

		CROSS-SECTION						PANEL		
		1972	1974	1976	1978	1980	1982	1972	1974	1976
		Men						Men		
1	(Egalitarian)	33*	34	34	42	35	37	33	34	33
2,3		18	20	25	21	27	24	21	21	26
4	(Neutral)	18	20	18	16	15	20	19	21	19
5,6		12	13	15	13	17	12	13	14	14
7	(Traditional)	18	13	9	8	6	6	15	9	9
n		1087	609	713	955	565	573	472	472	472
		Employed women						Employed women		
1	(Egalitarian)	38	40	37	49	40	47	42	44	34
2,3		16	19	26	19	29	23	20	21	27
4	(Neutral)	25	21	19	16	16	17	21	22	21
5,6		9	12	12	9	9	9	9	10	13
7	(Traditional)	13	8	6	7	5	5	9	4	6
n		579	359	441	562	372	349	176	176	176
	% of sampled women	39	41	42	48	50	48			
		Housewives						Housewives		
1	(Egalitarian)	25	21	24	26	27	29	25	26	29
2,3		14	19	13	15	27	18	14	18	12
4	(Neutral)	21	23	25	24	17	19	21	20	20
5,6		11	17	16	17	18	14	12	21	19
7	(Traditional)	29	20	23	18	12	19	29	16	20
n		672	334	374	406	196	202	165	165	165
	% of sampled women	47	45	37	34	27	28			

*All entries are percentages. Columns may not sum to 100 because of rounding.

TABLE B.2
Attitudes of Men, Employed Women, and Housewives by Education on an Equal Role for Women

	High school						Some college						College					
	1972	1974	1976	1978	1980	1982	1972	1974	1976	1978	1980	1982	1972	1974	1976	1978	1980	1982
MEN																		
1 (Egalitarian)	33*	32	31	39	32	30	31	38	33	43	40	44	38	35	40	49	37	47
2,3	12	15	18	16	20	18	23	21	31	29	32	35	27	36	36	27	40	27
4 (Neutral)	17	22	20	18	17	27	22	18	17	15	14	11	15	13	14	10	12	17
5,6	12	14	17	14	22	15	10	13	13	10	12	8	16	11	9	12	11	10
7 (Traditional)	25	16	13	13	9	11	13	10	5	3	3	4	4	6	1	1	0	0
n	561	392	410	552	297	294	342	105	138	194	136	142	184	109	163	207	129	137
EMPLOYED WOMEN																		
1 (Egalitarian)	32	33	29	44	28	45	42	46	48	53	51	43	49	55	53	64	59	58
2,3	12	16	24	17	30	19	19	19	27	25	26	25	22	29	31	20	29	28
4 (Neutral)	27	24	34	19	21	19	25	18	16	13	14	17	18	10	7	10	6	11
5,6	10	15	15	11	12	11	7	10	7	7	7	11	7	5	7	3	5	3
7 (Traditional)	19	11	8	9	9	7	7	6	2	2	2	4	3	0	1	3	0	0
n	298	233	274	343	207	166	192	67	86	126	87	111	89	58	81	92	78	72
HOUSEWIVES																		
1 (Egalitarian)	23	18	21	24	22	26	30	37	31	26	42	35	41	29	31	41	42	38
2,3	11	17	10	12	26	14	17	22	22	21	33	29	24	25	28	26	17	29
4 (Neutral)	22	25	25	25	18	19	22	18	25	24	11	15	15	14	26	15	25	25
5,6	11	15	16	17	20	17	14	16	16	18	8	15	11	32	11	10	17	0
7 (Traditional)	34	25	28	21	14	24	17	6	6	11	6	6	9	0	5	8	0	8
n	483	255	283	293	148	144	133	49	51	72	36	34	54	28	39	39	12	24

*All entries are percentages. Columns may not sum to 100 due to rounding error.

TABLE B.3
Distribution of Responses on Women's Seven-Point Equal-Role Scale by Awareness and Sex

		Men		Employed women		Housewives	
		Aware	Unaware	Aware	Unaware	Aware	Unaware
		1972					
Equal role	1	28.4*	35.6	50.6	33.5	43.1	22.3
	2,3	27.9	17.2	23.4	13.7	15.9	13.3
	4	16.6	19.8	14.3	26.9	6.8	23.2
	5,6	15.9	10.6	3.9	11.0	9.0	11.2
Place in home	7	11.2	16.8	7.8	14.8	25.0	30.0
n		169	303	77	182	44	233
% aware		35.8		29.7		15.9	
		1974					
Equal role	1	31.7	34.7	48.7	39.6	52.3	23.6
	2,3	28.7	18.0	28.9	15.6	13.6	19.6
	4	17.7	22.4	10.5	22.2	11.4	22.1
	5,6	16.5	12.3	7.9	12.7	15.9	17.0
Place in home	7	5.5	12.6	3.9	9.9	6.8	17.7
n		169	303	77	182	44	233
		1976					
Equal role	1	33.1	32.3	40.3	30.2	38.7	25.8
	2,3	26.1	25.7	31.2	23.0	20.5	13.7
	4	23.1	17.2	16.9	23.6	4.5	23.6
	5,6	12.5	14.2	7.8	15.4	27.3	15.5
Place in home	7	5.3	10.6	3.9	7.7	9.1	21.9
n		169	303	77	182	44	233

*All entries are percentages. Columns may not sum to 100 due to rounding errors.

TABLE B.4
Mean Thermometer Values for Aware and Unaware Groups by Sex

| | Aware | | | Unaware | | |
	Men	Employed women	Housewives	Men	Employed women	Housewives
			1972			
Mean	47.3	55.5	46.3	45.8	42.8	39.5
n	168	77	44	293	179	210
			1974			
Mean	53.5	60.4	58.0	52.7	48.0	50.0
n	168	77	44	293	179	210
			1976			
Mean	51.5	59.2	55.3	53.2	53.6	49.4
n	168	77	44	293	179	210

working with *responses, not respondents* in Table B.5. A response is a *pair* of answers to the *same* question—one answer in 1972 and one in 1976. Thus a respondent could have up to five responses (i.e., answer the five questions in both years). Finally, each respondent can be either pro/pro, pro/anti, anti/pro, or anti/anti—hence, the format of Table B.5.

The five attitude questions were variables 844, 846, 850, 852, and 854 in 1972 and 3,802, 3,804, 3,808, 3,809, and 3,811 in 1976 respectively. For each of the five attitude questions, respondents were presented with two statements and were asked "which of these two statements do you agree with the most?" We will list the five questions by their 1972 variable numbers with our coding of pro-/antifeminist.

VAR 844: "Many qualified women can't get good jobs; men with the same skills have much less trouble." (Pro)
"In general, men are more qualified than women for jobs that have great responsibility." (Anti)
VAR 846: "Women can best overcome discrimination by pursuing their individual career goals in as feminine a way as possible." (Anti)

TABLE B.5
Total Pro- and Antifeminist Responses to Five Attitude Questions for Aware and Unaware Groups by Sex

AWARE

	Men 1976			Employed women 1976			Housewives 1976		
	Pro	Anti		Pro	Anti		Pro	Anti	
1972 Pro	36.8	10.7	47.5	47.6	9.6	57.2	37.1	10.2	47.3
1972 Anti	15.6	36.9	52.5	15.9	26.9	42.8	18.5	34.2	52.7
	52.4	47.6	100.0	63.5	36.5	36.5	55.6	44.4	100.0
			(774)[a]			(353)			(205)

UNAWARE

	Men 1976			Employed women 1976			Housewives 1976		
	Pro	Anti		Pro	Anti		Pro	Anti	
1972 Pro	25.0	13.0	38.0	28.3	12.1	40.4	23.5	11.0	34.5
1972 Anti	19.0	43.0	62.0	17.4	42.2	59.6	18.7	46.8	65.5
	44.0	56.0	100.0	45.7	54.3	100.0	42.2	57.8	100.0
			(1631)			(904)			(1201)

[a] Total number of responses. Divide this number by five to get the approximate number of respondents in each category.

Appendix B / 189

"It is not enough for a woman to be successful herself; women must work together to change laws and customs that are unfair to all women." (Pro)

VAR 850: "It's more natural for men to have the top responsible jobs in the country." (Anti)

"Sex discrimination keeps women from the top jobs." (Pro)

VAR 852: "The best way to handle problems of discrimination is for each woman to make sure she gets the best training possible for what she wants to do." (Anti)

"Only if women organize and work together can anything really be done about discrimination." (Pro)

VAR 854: "By nature women are happiest when they are making a home and caring for children." (Anti)

"Our society, not nature, teaches women to prefer homemaking to work outside the home." (Pro)

Index

Abortion, 7
  Anderson, John and, 76-77
  attitudes toward, 84
  Carter, Jimmy and, 72, 75-77
  Congressional women and, 169-170
  ideology and, 96, 106-107
  issue priorities 55, 56, 57
  legalization of, 12
  nonvoters and, 142, 147
  Presidential politics and, 72, 75-77, 85
  Reagan, Ronald and, 42, 75-77, 82-84, 106
  voter behavior and, 58, 59
  women's opposition to, 37
Affirmative action, 12, 32
Age differences, 122-123
Alcoholism, 27-28
Aldrich, John, 179
Andersen, Kristi, 121, 136
Anderson, John, 50, 52
  discrimination and, 73
  fundamentalism and, 78
  Moral Majority and, 82
  nuclear power issue and, 71-72
  trust and, 136
  women's cohesiveness and, 56
Antifeminist movement, 37-38
Approval ratings (presidential), 53
Arms control, 114
Awareness, 31-38

Baxter, Sandra, 65, 68, 136
Beedy, Carrol, 159
Blacks
  earnings of, 5
  group cohesion and, 41-42
  See also Minorities; Racial discrimination
Boles, Janet, 2
Brown, Jerry, 59
Bullock, Charles S., III, 156
Busing
  Congressional women and, 170-171
  ideology and, 111
  issue attitudes and, 69
  voter behavior and, 58, 59

Campaign activities, 123-127
Carden, Maren L., 20
Carter, Jimmy, 4, 43, 44, 45, 53, 127
  campaign of, 48
  consumerism and, 162-163
  defeat of, 50-51, 52, 60, 77, 79-84
  discrimination and, 73-74
  environment and, 69
  equality and, 72-73
  fundamentalism and, 77-79
  government spending and, 61
  inflation and, 63-64
  nonvoters and, 142
  nuclear power and, 70-72
  Soviet-U.S. relations and, 66-68
  tax policy and, 64-65
  trusts and, 135-136
  voter behavior and, 57-60
Cavanagh, Thomas, 121-122
CBS/New York Times poll, 16, 53
Child care, 5-6, 30
  See also Family; Housewives; Sex role
Civil Rights Act, 2
Civil rights movement
  consciousness raising and, 26
  dissatisfaction and, 25
  family and, 16
  ideology and, 96
Comission on the Status of Women, 2
Communism, 31-32
Congressional women, 151-177
  ideology and, 153-156
  party loyalty and, 156-157
  regulation and, 162-164
Congress of United Women, 15
Conservatives and conservatism
  civil rights and, 96
  equality and, 99
  women and, 43-45
  See also Ideology
Constraint, 31-38
Consumerism, 162-164
Converse, Philip, 31-32
Cynicism, 128-132

Davis-Bacon Act, 164
Defense spending
  attitudes toward, 87-88
  Congressional women and, 165-168
  issue attitudes and, 67, 68
  issue priorities and, 55, 56
  Reagan, Ronald and, 79, 87-88
  voter behavior and, 58, 59
  See also Government spending; Soviet-U.S. relations
Democratic party
  defeat of, 82
  government spending and, 86
  issues and, 158
  participation in, 127
  voter turnout and, 140, 142
  See also Party politics
Diffusion, 31-38
Discrimination, 1
  Equal Rights Amendment and, 74
  ideology and, 96, 104-105
  legitimacy in, 2
  nonvoters and, 142
  Presidential politics and, 73-74
  satisfaction levels and, 25-26
Draft registration, 6-7

Education (of women)
  abortion and, 106-107
  awareness and, 36-37
  busing and, 111
  constraint and, 34-35
  discrimination and, 104-105
  efficacy and, 138-140
  employment and, 13-14, 18-19
  environmentalism and, 116
  equality and, 13-20, 72-73, 100
  Equal Rights Amendment and, 107
  feminism and, 17-18, 34
  jobs programs and, 112
  liberalism and, 16-17
  minorities and, 112
  nonvoters and, 140
  nuclear power and, 115
  political participation and, 126-127
  Presidential politics and, 46, 48-49
  Reagan, Ronald and, 51-52
  school prayer and, 110
  Soviet-U.S. relations and, 113
  trust and, 131-132
  voting preferences and, 45-46
  women's liberation movement and, 22-24, 102, 103
Efficacy, 136-140
Egalitarianism. *See* Equality
Eisenhower, Dwight David, 53, 154, 166

Employment (of women)
  abortion and, 75-76, 84, 106, 107
  Anderson, John and, 50
  awareness and, 33, 35
  busing and, 111
  campaign activities and, 123-127
  Congressional women and, 156
  discrimination and, 73-74, 104, 105
  education and, 13-14, 18-19
  efficacy and, 136, 137-138
  environmentalism and, 116
  equality and, 9-13, 18, 24, 72-73, 85, 99
  Equal Rights Amendment and, 74-75, 107-109
  feminism and, 10-11, 28
  fundamentalism and, 78
  gender gap and, 89-92
  government spending and, 61
  ideology and, 117
  increase in, 42
  issue priorities and, 56-57
  jobs programs and, 80, 112
  liberalism and, 65
  minorities and, 69, 81, 82, 111-112
  nuclear power and, 115
  Presidential politics and, 49-50
  satisfaction in, 25-31
  school prayer and, 110
  segregation in, 13
  Soviet-U.S. relations and, 65-68, 113
  tax policy and, 65
  trust/cynicism and, 129, 130, 134
  voter participation and, 42-43
  voter preferences and, 45
  welfare and, 62
  women's liberation movement and, 21-24, 102
Environmentalism
  ideology and, 116
  issue attitudes and, 69-70
  voter behavior and, 58, 59
Epstein, Cynthia, 15
Equality
  awareness and, 32-34
  Congressional women and, 168-169
  education and, 13-20
  employment and, 9-13, 18
  ideology and, 98-101
  issue priorities and, 54-56, 57
  methodology and, 183-189
  nonvoters and, 142-144
  Presidential politics and, 72-73, 85
  social class and, 15
  voter behavior and, 58, 59
Equal Rights Amendment (ERA), 2
  Anderson, John and, 74

awareness and, 32
Carter, Jimmy and, 74-75, 85, 108
Congressional women and, 168-169
Hart, Gary and, 88-89
ideology and, 107-109
issue priorities and, 54
men and, 19
National Organization for Women and, 7
nonvoters and, 144-145
Presidential politics and, 12, 74-75
Reagan, Ronald and, 42, 72, 74-75, 108
social issues and, 97
voter behavior and, 58, 59
women's opposition to, 2, 4, 15, 31, 37

Family
feminism and, 15-16, 38
New Right and, 82
sex role and, 3, 26-27
Social Security system and, 37
women's movement and, 12
Feminism and feminist movement
antifeminist movement and, 37-38
awareness/diffusion/restraint paradigm, 31-38
consciousness raising, 26
diffusion of, 53
education and, 17-18, 34
employment and, 8, 10-11, 28
family and, 15-16, 38
housewives and, 8, 42
McGovern, George and, 46
Presidential politics and, 12
self-esteem and, 12-13
social class and, 14-15, 19-20
women's suffrage and, 1-2
See also Women's liberation movement
Food Stamp program, 159-161
Ford, Gerald, 43, 44, 45, 48, 50, 53, 127, 163
Foreign policy. *See* Defense spending; Soviet-U.S. relations
Frankovic, Kathleen A., 92, 156
Freeman, Jo, 1-2, 17, 20
Friedan, Betty, 38
Fundamentalism, 77-79, 82, 142

Gallup poll, 17, 83
Gehlen, Frieda, 161
Gender gap
congressional politics and, 86-92
future and, 86-92
nonvoters and, 144-147
Glazer, Nora, 3
Goldwater, Barry, 37, 79, 84n
Government spending
attitudes toward, 87

issue attitudes, 60-61
issue priorities, 55, 56
nonvoters and, 141, 142, 144, 146
Reagan, Ronald and, 60-61, 79, 84, 86
trust/cynicism and, 134
voter behavior and, 57-59
See also Defense spending
Group cohesiveness
housewives and, 59-60
ideology and, 116
suffrage and, 41
Group consciousness, 4-5

Hart, Gary, 88-89
Hawkins, Paula, 152
Hays, Patricia Lee Findley, 156
Homosexuality, 96, 172
Hoover, Herbert, 159
Horizontal diffusion, 37
House of Representatives, 153-156
Housewives
abortion and, 75-76, 84, 106, 107
awareness and, 33, 34, 35
busing and, 111
campaign activities and, 123-127
cohesiveness of, 59-60
constraint and, 34
decrease in, 42, 53
discrimination and, 73-74
efficacy and, 138
environment and, 69, 116
equality and, 9-13, 18, 72-73, 99
Equal Rights Amendment and, 74-75, 107-109
feminism and, 8
fundamentalism and, 78
gender gap and, 89-92
government spending and, 61
issue priorities and, 56-57
jobs programs and, 80, 112
minorities and, 69, 81, 82, 112
Nixon, Richard and, 127
nonvoters and, 142
nuclear power and, 115
Presidential politics and, 47-48, 50
Reagan, Ronald and, 50-51
Republican party and, 128
satisfaction level and, 27-28
Soviet-U.S. relations and, 65-68, 113
tax policy and, 65
trust/cynicism and, 130, 132
voter participation and, 42-43
voting preferences of, 45
welfare and, 62
women's liberation movement and, 22, 24, 102

Huddleston, George, 159
Humphrey, Hubert, 43, 44, 45, 46, 127
Hyde amendment, 12

Ideology, 95-120
  consistency in, 117-119
  spectrum in, 95-96
  See also entries under names of specific issues
Inflation
  issue attitudes and, 63-64
  issue priorities and, 54, 55, 56, 57
  voter behavior and, 58, 59

Jackson, Henry, 165
Jobs programs
  Congressional women and, 161-162
  ideology and, 112
  Reagan, Ronald and, 79-82
  See also Welfare
Johnson, Lyndon B., 53, 79, 154

Kassenbaum, Nancy, 152
Kemp-Roth tax reduction plan, 64
Kennedy, Edward, 142
Kennedy, John F., 2, 53, 129, 165
Kirkpatrick, Jeane, 17
Korean war, 53, 65

Labor force, 7-8
  See also Employment (of women)
Labor unions
  Congressional women and, 164
  group cohesiveness and, 4, 42
Lansing, Marjorie, 65, 68, 136
League of Women Voters, 2
Legitimate discrimination, 2
Liberals and liberalism
  civil rights and, 96
  Congressional women, 154-156
  education and, 16-17
  employment and, 45, 65
  equality and, 99
  ideology and, 95-96
  women and, 43-45
  See also Ideology

Macoby, Eleanore, 6
Marriage
  satisfaction and, 30-31
  sex role and, 3
  stigma and, 15
Marxism, 31, 159
Mayors, 151-152
McCourt, Kathleen, 20
McGovern, George, 4, 12, 17, 43, 47-48, 127
  feminism and, 46

women and, 42, 128
McKelvey, Richard D., 179
Mead, Margaret, 15
Media, 7
  Carter, Jimmy and, 48
  gender gap and, 88
  Presidential politics and, 127
  Reagan, Ronald and, 134
  sex role and, 2-3
  voter behavior and, 59
Men
  abortion and, 76, 85
  awareness and, 33, 34, 35
  Carter, Jimmy and, 50
  Carter/Reagan election, 51-53
  child care and, 5-6
  conservative/liberal preferences, 43-45
  discrimination issue and, 105
  equality and, 24, 99, 100
  Equal Rights Amendment and, 19, 109
  group cohesiveness and, 4
  ideology and, 117
  minorities and, 112
  nonvoters and, 142
  political participation and, 124
  Presidential politics and, 46-47, 48-49
  stability and, 36
  trust/cynicism and, 129, 130
  voter participation and, 43
  women's liberation movement and, 22, 23, 24
  See also Sex differences; Sex role
Minorities
  discrimination against, 2
  ideology and, 111-112
  issue attitudes and, 68-69
  issue priorities and, 55, 56
  Reagan, Ronald and, 79-82
  voter behavior and, 58, 59

National Association of Business and Professional Women, 2
National Organization for Women (NOW), 2
  Equal Rights Amendment and, 7
  membership of, 15
  Reagan, Ronald and, 45
National Women's Party, 2
Neuberger, Maureen, 152
New Deal, 95, 98, 158, 161, 162
New Right, 84
  abortion and, 106
  busing and, 111
  Reagan, Ronald and, 82
  voter behavior and, 59
New York Times/CBS poll, 16, 53
Nixon, Richard, 43, 44, 45, 46, 47, 48, 53, 154
  housewives and, 127

mandate and, 79
Nonvoters, 140-147
Nuclear power
 Congressional women and, 167
 ideology and, 114-115
 issue attitudes, 70-72
 nonvoters and, 142
 Presidential politics and, 85
 voter behavior and, 58, 59

Oberschall, Anthony, 14
Occupational Safety and Health Administration (OSHA), 162
Oil prices, 58, 59

Party politics
 Congressional elections, 45
 Congressional women and, 152, 154, 156-157
 gender gap and, 89-92
 group cohesion and, 41-42
 ideology and, 97-98
 political participation and, 127-129
 sex role and, 3
 suffrage and, 41
 voter turnout and, 140, 142
 women and, 4, 50
 women's liberation movement and, 102-103
 See also Democratic party; Republican party
Peace movement, 6, 65-68
Political participation, 121-150
 campaign activities, 123-127
 efficacy criteria and, 136-140
 gender differences in, 121-122
 nonparticipants, 140-147
 party politics and, 127-129
 persuasion factor, 125
 trust/cynicism, 129-134, 135-136
Presidential politics
 abortion and, 75-77
 Carter, Jimmy and, 48-49
 Carter/Reagan election, 50-54
 conservative/liberal preferences, 43-45
 discrimination and, 73-74
 education and, 45-46
 employment and, 45
 equality and, 72-73
 Equal Rights Amendment and, 108
 feminism and, 12
 fundamentalism and, 77-79
 housewives and, 47-48
 issue attitudes, 60-79
 issue priorities in, 54-57
 political participation and, 121-122, 127
 sex differences and, 85

 social issues and, 97-98
 voter behavior and, 57-60
 voter participation and, 42-43
 women's liberation movement and, 97
Primary system, 48, 127

Racial discrimination, 1, 16
 response to, 3
 sex discrimination compared, 3-4
 See also Blacks; Discrimination; Minorities
Reagan, Ronald, 4, 43, 45, 154
 appeal of, 82
 approval ratings of, 53
 discrimination and, 73-74
 election of, 50-51
 environmentalism and, 69-70
 equality and, 72-73, 100
 fundmentalism and, 77-79
 ideology and, 96
 inflation and, 63-64
 mandate of, 79-84
 New Right and, 110
 nuclear power and, 70-72
 social issues and, 42
 Soviet-U.S. relations and, 113-114
 tax policy and, 64-65
 trust/cynicism and, 134, 135-136
 voter behavior and, 57-60
 welfare and, 159
 women's role and, 72
 women's support for, 128
Regulation, 162-164
Relative deprivation, 20, 28
Religion, 78-79
 See also Fundamentalism
Republican party
 nonvoters and, 142
 participation and, 128-129
 regulation and, 162-163
 social issues and, 158
 See also Party politics
Roe v. Wade, 106, 169
Roosevelt, Franklin D., 4, 158

Sapiro, Virginia, 7, 12, 92
Satisfaction, 25-31
Schlafly, Phyllis, 12, 31, 37, 102
School prayer
 Congressional women and, 172
 ideology and, 110
 New Right and, 82
 Presidential politics and, 78-79
 Reagan, Ronald and, 84
 voter behavior and, 58, 59
Sex differences
 abortion and, 84
 arms control and, 114

Sex differences (continued)
 defense spending and, 88, 166
 educaiton and, 18-19
 environment and, 69-70, 116
 gender gap and, 92
 ideology and, 117
 issue priorities, 56-57
 nuclear power and, 114-115
 political participation and, 125
 political patterns and, 54
 Presidential politics and, 85
 Soviet-U.S. relations and, 65-68, 113
 trust/cynicism and, 132-133, 136
 voter turnout and, 121-122
Sex role
 child care and, 5-6
 employment and, 8
 employment satisfaction and, 25
 family and, 26-27
 feminism and, 16
 media and, 2-3
 Reagan, Ronald and, 72
 satisfaction and, 28-30
Singleness, 15, 30-31
Smith, Margaret Chase, 152
Social Darwinism, 62, 86-87
Social Security system, 37, 84
Soviet-U.S. relations
 ideology and, 113-114
 issue attitudes, 66-68, 98
 issue priorities and, 55, 56
 nonvoters and, 142
 voter behavior and, 58, 59
 See also Defense spending
Stereotyping, 2, 5-6
Stockman, David, 60
STOP-ERA organization, 37
Suffrage, 1-2, 41
Supply-side economics, 64
Survey Research Center, 8-9, 21

Tax policy
 issue attitudes, 64-65
 issue priorities, 55, 56, 57
 Reagan, Ronald and, 84
 voter behavior and, 58, 59

 waste and, 134
Television, 2-3
 See also Media
Truman, David, 4, 5
Trust (in government)
 cynicism and, 128-132
 political participation and, 135-136
 sex differences and, 132-133

Unemployment
 issue attitudes, 63-64

Values, 16-17
Vertical diffusion, 37
Vietnam war, 53, 65, 79, 129, 154, 165-166
Voter behavior, 57-60
Voter turnout
 party politics and, 140, 142
 trust and, 135
 See also Political participation

Wallace, George, 4, 17, 43n, 44, 45
Watergate scandal, 124, 129
Welch, Susan, 125
Welfare
 Congressional women and, 158-161
 ideology and, 111-112
 issue attitudes and, 61-62
 issue priorities and, 55
 Reagan, Ronald and, 79-82
 voter behavior and, 58, 59
Women
 discrimination against, 1
 diversity among, 7
 employment experience of, 7-13
 group cohesion among, 41-42
Women's liberation movement
 family and, 12
 ideology and, 101-103
 Presidential politics and, 97
 support for, 20-24
 See also Feminism and feminist movement
Women's suffrage, 1-2

Yankelovich, Daniel, 16-17